Act Like You've Been There

RULES FOR MY BROTHER

NICK FOLEY

Edited by Paul Bramley and Dana Throop.
Cover Design by Andruw Belanger.

Library and Archives Canada Cataloguing in Publication

CIP data on file with the National Library and Archives

ISBN 978-0-9868889-0-8

Contact Nick at: rulesformybro@hotmail.com
And
On twitter at:
@rulesformybro

CONTENTS

FOREWORD

I am truly honoured to write the foreword to *Act Like You Have Been There: Rules for my Brother*. Nick and I are cousins, friends and at one time co-workers. Nick inspires me with his passion for life and his dedication to follow his dreams. Nick has always told me that he wishes that he could have shared more of his life lessons with his younger brother as Nick moved away from home at such a young age to follow his hockey dreams. What Nick doesn't realize is that he inspired his younger brother and many others with his incredible perseverance and determination to be successful in life.

Nick is an extremely successful person with many gifts and talents to offer. He is not only an incredible and gifted writer. He is holds a Bachelor of History degree from St. Mary's University, he has his Bachelor of Education with Honours degree from The University of Main and is a certified teacher, specializing in teaching Behavioural Youth. He has created the Bayfield Random Acts of Kindness Program, which encourages troubled youth to live to a higher standard, by doing nice things randomly, to strangers. Nick is a successful Web Entrepreneur and a captivating public speaker. Nick also the founder of *The Celebrate The Hero Campaign,* which is an initiative he has been taking into the local schools to promote positive actions and reducing the use of intimidation and replacing it with positive interactions amongst others. Nick had an incredible four year Ontario Hockey League Experience and was a two time humanitarian of the year nominee. Nick was also a four year varsity athlete on Hockey Scholarship.

I was so thrilled when Nick pursued his goal to write *Act Like You Have Been There: Rules for my Brother* as he is always offering his anecdotes to family and friends. Throughout his life journey Nick has been reflecting on what he believes are the essential rules that are vital in life. An excellent example of this is when I watched Nick with my daughter who was three years old at the time. Nick was sitting with her on his lap and telling her that she is an incredible person with lots of great things to offer this world. He reached into his pocket and gave her a rock with the word: *COURAGE* on it. He told her that whenever she was scared or needed strength she was to hold the rock tight and his courage and strength would be with her. I was so touched by his gesture and she still has the rock beside her bed every night and draws strength from it. I will find it in her school bag or with her at her skating competitions.

Act Like You Have Been There: Rules for my Brother deals with the important things in life. We live in a time where we are over-worked and never seem to take the opportunity to appreciate our true blessings. This book has excellent advice and guidance for the journey of life. This is the only chance we have at life and we should live it to the fullest. *Act Like You Have Been There: Rules for my Brother* can be utilized for every member of the family. It is an excellent tool to assist parents with teaching the fundamentals of life. It is very evident that Nicholas was raised with strong values and morals.

Act Like You Have Been There: Rules for my Brother offers insight on such important virtues and life lessons; some topics of what this incredible book covers are: *Live with integrity, conviction, strength and courage, Accept who you are, Be Accountable, Courtesy gets you everywhere.*

As a college professor and a life skills facilitator this books allows me the opportunity and platform to discuss and provide advice on the qualities we have within that are critical in being successful in having a happy and fulfilling life with no regrets.

I hope that Act *Like You Have Been There: Rules for my Brother* will give you something to think about while on your life journey and will allow you to live to your fullest potential. It definitely has given me more passion for life and the desire to give something back and become something more.

Love Lori
Lori LaMorre-Slatter
Professor/Field Placement Coordinator Social Service Worker Program Loyalist College
Life Skills Facilitator

INTRODUCTION

Act Like You Have Been There: Rules for My Brother began many years ago, as a set of rules for my little brother to follow, while I was living away from home. I jotted down on a piece of paper a few things that I felt he needed to understand. Little things he could refer to in case he needed guidance during a difficult time. It started as a few thoughts like: always have a firm handshake, enter a room with confidence, live with chivalry. It has since developed into a large collection of rules and words of advice.

I often wondered, if this question was asked to others, how would they respond? "If you had one word of advice to leave your brother, what would it be?" I figured if this advice could apply to one person, it could certainly apply to many. There was no criterion to whom the question was posed: colleagues, friends, family and strangers were all met with my question. If they answered, I wrote it down. If I felt there was a message, I used it.

This has been an ongoing project for quite some time; have I lived by these rules every day of my life? The answer to that question is no. Perhaps that is why I have not been able to write this until now. I have made some mistakes but as a smart friend once told me, "it is only a mistake if you do not learn from it." I can definitely say that although some of the mistakes I have made in my life, I have made more than once, the one thing I do know for sure, I learned from them.

My hope is that you will get as much out of reading this project, as I did writing it.

Nick

PART ONE

PROFESSIONAL MOTIVATIONS & TRUTHS

ACT LIKE YOU HAVE BEEN THERE

"It's not who you are that holds you back,
it's who you think you aren't."
– Author Unknown

Dear brother,

I have spent as long as I can remember, telling people to act like they have been there. I am not sure exactly, where and when I heard that expression or if I just made it up. I know for sure that this expression has been a fixture in the dialogue, my friends and I have adopted over the years because of its very real meaning. I think that it is popular among us because it holds true, no matter where you are or what you are doing, literally and metaphorically.

Quite simply, act like you been there means have confidence in what you are doing. If you experience success, do not gloat or flaunt it. Be respectful, humble, and courteous. Remember in some cases, your success may mean someone else has failed: think about that when hearing good news. It is important to be gracious in defeat and respectful in victory.

Do not under any circumstances be intimidated. No person, no matter what they have done or do, is better then you. So remember, do not be intimidated by other people's success. They are not superior. You are in the same room as that person because you deserve to be. I remember walking into a green room, back stage before a variety show performance I was taking part in and I saw Andy Kim, a rock star who has sold millions of records over decades, and other successful bands that were starting to accumulate a real following, all of whom were waiting to go on stage throughout the night.

When I walked into that room I felt like a fan and I felt like I did not belong, as the band members only looked at me briefly before getting back to what they were doing. I immediately walked out, went to my car and told myself to start acting like I have been there before. I walked back into that room with confidence and purpose and with a sense of belonging. It was not long before I was socializing with the members of the other acts and feeling like I did belong. I began to feel better about what I was doing and who I was, and that confidence showed in my performance.

Acting like you have been there encompasses how you act when out in public as well. I understand the importance of having fun and creating memories with your friends, but remember, whether you are at a fancy restaurant or a pub with your buddies, handle yourself with class and integrity.

You may be presented with a situation, where you are meeting someone who has status in the community or even the country, where you live. When doing so, handle yourself with confidence. Walk into the room where the meeting will take place like you have been there before. Be gracious and courteous yes, but do not be meek. It is a privilege but when you are looking back at your experience, you want to be able to look back at it and think, "I handled that situation, with confidence, as though I have been there before." By doing so, the experience will be a far more rewarding one.

Acting like you've been there has been a consistent motto of mine, for as long as I can remember. I reflect upon it, in almost every situation I have been presented with in my life. It reminds me to be confident in who I am, in what I am doing and in what I have accomplished. It reminds me to handle myself with character and with integrity. It reminds me to be respectful, courteous, and gracious. Above all, it reminds me to be me and to be happy with that.

Act like you have been there.

Nick

Always Wear a Suit to an Interview

"Clothes make the man.
Naked people have little or no influence on society."
–Mark Twain

Dear brother,

It is always important to wear a suit to an interview. Wearing a suit to an interview, shows the employer that you are serious about the job and I strongly believe, first impressions start with your appearance. Before you say anything, wearing a suit automatically shows the employer that you are taking this opportunity seriously. It also shows that you take pride in your appearance, how you are perceived, and that you are looking to be the successful candidate for the position.

Our cousin Brandon told me a story once about wearing a suit to an interview. He went to an interview when he was fresh out of college. He wore the suit that he had purchased for the purpose of job hunting. When he got to this particular interview, both he and the person conducting the interview realized early on that he did not have enough experience for the position. He thanked the prospective employer for his time and walked toward the door to exit the room. As he got to the door the gentlemen behind the desk said, "Hey kid, nice suit."

As he was driving home his phone rang, it was the gentlemen from the office he had just left. He called him to ask, if he would he be interested in another position with the same company? Would he come back tomorrow and interview with his colleague? Brandon accepted, went back and was offered the position.

Brandon cannot say for sure if it was the suit that got him the other interview, but one thing is for sure, wearing it didn't hurt. The point is, take pride in how you look, especially at interviews. If you conduct yourself with confidence, and look as though you are ready to be a part of the organization you are interviewing for, you will have a better chance at leaving a good impression.

Always wear a suit to an interview.

Nick

ASK QUESTIONS

"People who ask confidently get more than those who are
hesitant and uncertain. When you figured out what you
want to ask for, do it with certainty, boldness and confidence."
— Jack Canfield

Dear brother,

It is often said that there is no such thing as a stupid question. If you do not know the answer to something, do not hesitate to ask. Be the metaphorical sponge that soaks up as much knowledge as you can. Too often people will stick with what they know, and will not attempt to broaden their horizons, by seeking the answer to the questions they want to ask, for fear of what they will find out.

Many times in my life, I did not take advantage of opportunities to ask questions. In school, I really struggled with math. Every day I would go to math class and sit in silence, as I watched my teacher facilitate the lesson on the board. I would try to understand what the teacher was teaching but I just couldn't understand it. In most cases, I figured out just enough to pass but as the grades got higher, the math got harder and I grew more and more frustrated. Eventually, I just stopped taking the subject all together because of my lack of success. Now I kick myself, because the reason I avoided math was because I was not successful. I equate this lack of progression not to any teacher, but to the fact I refused to ask questions.

Be curious. It is okay to ponder questions and do what you can to find answers to them. Life is full of questions, which should be answered or at least asked. Knowledge, no matter what the capacity, is power, and the best way to earn that knowledge is by asking questions, even the tough ones, no matter what they are.

Ask questions.

Nick

BE A LEADER

"A leader is one who knows the way,
goes the way, and shows the way."
— John Maxwell

Dear brother,

Lead the way even when it is easier to follow. Life is going to present you with many situations, when it is easier to follow the crowd and do the same thing as everyone else. I do not think a person is a born leader, I also do not think that leadership should be appointed. I believe in order to be a leader, you have to earn it. You earn leadership through your actions. Can you motivate through words? Yes. However, actions are what make a good leader different from the rest; actions are what make a leader worth following. Anyone can talk. It is how you act that will make you a true leader.

Many men have made careers leading teams and organizations. Men like Vince Lombardi, the famous football coach of the Green Bay Packers, or Paul "Bear" Bryant, the charismatic head coach of the Alabama Crimson Tide are just two examples. These men led their teams to championships because they had a vision. They knew the goal they wanted to achieve and they accomplished it by holding their players accountable. Those men did not take short cuts in anything they did and they made sure, the teams that they coached executed a plan to its fullest extent, in order to accomplish the ultimate goal of victory.

I think having a vision, being accountable and executing a plan is a leadership model, which can be applied to a person's everyday life. It does not matter if you are in a leadership position or not.

Live your life with a plan and with substance. By living your life with a plan, people will look to you as a leader, as someone who leads by example and lives their life with a purpose. Be the man who makes his own decisions: the man who walks, talks, and lives with a sense of who they are. Be the man that can be relied on during a time of need, or counted on when things are not going well for others. Be there for your friends, family and loved ones through all their heartaches and triumphs. Be accountable. Do not waver when it comes to making the tough decisions. Be yourself.

Be a leader.

Nick

BE ON TIME

"Better to be three hours early than one minute too late."
— William Shakespeare

Dear brother,

Our cousin Kasey once told me, "if you are five minutes early, you are ten minutes late." I personally do not think you need to be that fanatical when it comes to being on time, however, I will say it is very important to be on time. When you are on time, it not only shows respect for what it is you are doing, it also shows respect for yourself and the people you work for. Being on time shows people that you are organized. It is very easy to be late, anyone can be late. And yes, sometimes in life things happen that you cannot control. I understand that, however, being late consistently shows disrespect for what you are doing. In work it shows your boss you do not take your position seriously, for meetings it shows your colleagues you do not value their time. On a date it shows the person you are not interested.

When you are working, it is important to arrive to work early and stay late sometimes. I remember at a young age, asking dad why he left for his job two hours before he had to be there. His response was simple, "Getting to work early shows everybody that you value and take your position seriously; putting in extra work is good for the soul and gives you a sense of accomplishment." This comes from the man, who for five years drove an hour to and from work and then started his own company and arrived at work, two hours before any of his employees. He knew the value of arriving on time. I have remembered his commitment and advice my entire life and have done my best to apply it to every job I have had.

I read an interesting quote from a book called "The Last Lecture," which really compounds dad's point. The author Randy Pausch wrote, "People ask me all the time how are you so successful, being tenured at such a young age?" His response is simple. "Call my office at ten o'clock on a Friday night and I will tell you."

That statement resonates true. Arriving to work early and staying late will get you noticed.

Be on time.

Nick

BE THE MOST PREPARED

"Success always comes when preparation meets opportunity."
– Henry Hartman

Dear brother,

Being smart is not just having cognitive knowledge about things that are happening in the world, or getting A's on a report card. In my opinion, being smart is being fully prepared for everything you do. Life can sometimes come at you quick, so arm yourself by being prepared for whatever life presents.

Life gives us situations, in which a person who comes prepared will achieve success. Interviews are a specific example. If you are applying for a job and get the opportunity to have an interview, you need to make sure you are prepared. Looking up information about the company is important. Remember to know exactly what the job that you are interviewing for consists of. Find out a little information about the history of the company. It is important to have a strong knowledge base, be yourself and answer questions honestly. Do not be afraid to ask questions. The more you are prepared; the more confident you will be. If you are confident and communicate your knowledge well, you will be successful in an interview every time.

I was doing a presentation once in a class I was in at University. It was a class on the History of the Modern Family from 1300 - 1700. It was a very small class, about twelve people in total, and as luck would have it, I was the only male. At the end of the term we had to deliver a thirty minute presentation on a topic we picked out of a hat. The topics ranged in scope and in time frame, but were centered around families. I pulled, "Sexual reproduction and practices." When I read it to the eleven other people in my class (who were all women, as I mentioned), they burst out laughing. I was mortified: I had no idea how I was going to pull this off. After some contemplation, I decided to prepare myself and become a bit of an "expert" on the subject. When I spoke in front of that room full of women, I knew everything I could about sexual reproduction and practices. I stood there for thirty minutes presenting and answering questions to the best of my ability. The reason I was able to pull it off is because I was prepared. I got an A by the way, and I am still pretty well versed on the practices back then.

Be prepared in life, when you awake every morning become one step closer to reaching your goal. You do not have to be the smartest, but it is important to be the most prepared.

Be the most prepared.

Nick

BE YOUR OWN MAN

"What other people think about you is not your concern."
— Marci Evans

Dear Brother,

It is important to be your own man and not to let other people manipulate you into doing things that you know are wrong. When you are young, it can be very easy to be manipulated into doing things you do not want to do. Sometimes these actions snowball and before you know what is happening, you have made one bad choice after another and you find it difficult to stop the downward momentum.

My thought is that if your instinct says that what you are doing is wrong, then it is. Trust your instincts. You have been raised right and you know the difference between right and wrong. At first, it may seem difficult to stop what you are doing. The people around you may give you a hard time, but at the end of the day you will be happy with the decision you have made. You have to live with you, remember that.

Conversely, if you want to do something you have been thinking about for a long time, then go and do it. Do not concern yourself or worry, what people will think about the decisions you make. Your decisions are your decisions and you answer to you. You may or may not be successful at whatever it is you attempt, however, you will always be able to say you have tried. I took chances and didn't always play it safe, but I lived my life the way I wanted to. It may sound cliché to say, but life is short. Live life and do all the things you want to do.

Be your own man.

Nick

Do Not Compromise Your Name for Anyone

"A good name, like good will, is attained by many actions and may be lost by one." —Anonymous

Dear brother,

I was given this poem from my university hockey coach, I feel it best exemplifies the point that I am trying to get across.

Family Name

You got it from your father
It was all he had to give
So it's yours to use and cherish
For as long as you may live
If you lost the watch he gave you
It can always be replaced;
But a black mark on your name
Can never be erased
It was clean the day you took it
And a worthy name to bear
When he got it from his father
There was no dishonor there
So make sure you guide it wisely
After all is said and done
You'll be glad the name is spotless
When you give it to your son
Anonymous

Do not compromise your name for anyone.
Nick

Do Not Put Off 'Till Tomorrow What Can Be Done Today

"It's not the things in life you do that you regret,
it's the things you don't do"
— Author unknown

Dear brother,

Life is short, so do not "get around to doing something," do it. I am sure you have heard many clichés, which go along with people telling you that life is short. The simple reality is that we have no idea, when our time on this earth is going to be up. Think about it: on your actual last day, whenever that may be, do you want to be longing for all the things you didn't do?

The only guarantee in life is, we are all going to die. Sometimes we know approximately when, sometimes we don't. In the mean time, I encourage you to do the things you want to do and live your life to the fullest. I know we are not made of money and sometimes going away on elaborate vacations, may not be an option. However, if you want that elaborate vacation then take steps in order to make it happen. Make the little sacrifices to make it a reality. You can control your path; it is your life.

I would encourage you to not leave things unsaid. If you have a friend you have not spoken to in some time, reach out. With the social media that is available to us in our life, losing communication with people should not ever be an option. Tell people how you feel, carrying things around inside you is not good for stress levels, which can lead to health complications. We do not know what day will be our last, so make sure you do more of the things you enjoy, and surround yourself with the people that make you the happiest.

Do not put off 'till tomorrow what can be done today.

Nick

Do Not Worry About What Could Have Been, Concentrate On What Is

"The one charm of the past is that it is in the past."—Oscar Wilde

Dear brother,

I remember seeing Gene for the first time and thinking to myself, she is the most beautiful woman I have ever seen. She was smart and witty and had a smile that would light up a room. Her hair was long, dark, and curly. She had a real zest for life. When she looked at you with her brown eyes, you suddenly didn't think of anything else in the world. When she spoke, she spoke with conviction, always choosing her words wisely. Her ideology was hers and if you didn't agree with it, she had no problems explaining to you why she thought the way she did. She enjoyed life, with all its trials and tribulations and accepted things as they came. She was easy going, a leader who had a real presence. I found myself staring at her often when we were together, wondering what I had done to deserve the admiration of a woman like this. She inspired to me to be better. She believed in me, when I didn't believe in myself. She was the most selfless and giving woman I have ever met. Her confidence and vulnerability were a perfect combination. In my opinion, she was the most beautiful woman in the world, and at one point she was in love with me.

You might be wondering what happened. What happened was that I had fallen in love with her as well, but it was too late. I did not realize when I was feeling those emotions, during the time we spent together that they were love and they were real, or did I realize that it was what I wanted. Time passed and my constant negative answers to her questions took their toll, along with some stupid mistakes, one compounding the other. She eventually decided to cut her losses and go her own way. When I tried to get her back, it was too late. It was hard for me to accept, and I found myself constantly asking what if? For a long time those questions consumed my existence.

One day a dear friend told me that I couldn't continue to live in the past. What was done was done. I had hurt her and she would now always have her guard up when it came to me. I needed to accept that, she told me. She continued, insisting my confession be my release and the key to start living in the present. My friend was right. If my love for this woman was that strong, I needed to let her live her life. She did not need the burden of a person in her past telling her how they felt. There was nothing good going to come from that, saying those things would not do anything for anyone.

Too many times in people's lives, they think about the past and wonder what could have been, if only they had acted or thought a bit differently. I have found the reality is that there is nothing you can do about the past but learn from it. If what you did in the past bothers you that much, then use it as a learning opportunity. Concentrate on what is happening around you now, so you do not make the same mistakes again. Be there for the people who are in your life at this moment. Remember the past, but don't live in it.

Don't not worry about what could have been, concentrate on what is.

Nick

IF YOU ARE GOING TO HOOT LIKE AN OWL AT NIGHT, YOU BETTER SOAR LIKE AN EAGLE IN THE MORNING

"It is easy to dodge our responsibilities, but we cannot dodge the consequences of dodging our responsibilities."
— Josiah Stamp

Dear brother,

Too often young people have a disregard for responsibility because they were out gallivanting with friends. I am not saying that going out with your buddies is not important to do. I know as well as anyone that male bonding, is a great time and a necessity. I would even argue that bonding with 'the boys' is an integral memory making time, which everyone in their life should experience. Anyone who knows me, knows that I value those times and have taken part in many nights of libations and light-hearted, memory making foolishness.

However, at the same time I am also here to tell you that the world does not stop the next day because you were out with your friends. I remember going out one night for a drink with a couple of guys. One drink turned into too many and before I knew it, it was almost three in the morning. Normally fine, however, I had a summer landscaping job that started every morning at six. When my alarm went off at five thirty I had a choice: call in sick, which is what I wanted to do, or show up, as I had a responsibility. I chose to show up. I am not sure how productive I was that day, in fact, I am sure my boss would argue that I was not at all, but at least I showed up.

My point is that life is full of impromptu situations, which sometimes turn into the best nights of your life. Take advantage of them from time to time but remember before doing so, life will continue in the morning and if you have responsibilities, you need to meet those responsibilities. As you get older, those responsibilities may include other people, it will not matter to young children that daddy was out with the boys.

If you are going to hoot like an owl at night, you better soar like an eagle in the morning.

Nick

Invest your Money

"Investors have very short memories." — Roman Abramovich

Dear brother,

Investing your money is very important. I cannot stress this enough. History shows that over time the cost of living will always go up. The result of doing nothing with your money over time will cause it to lose its buying power. There are many options that you can explore when trying to figure out where or how to invest. My advice is to invest with a company or a person that you feel comfortable doing so with.

It is your money, so when you are investing, ask questions, like:

1. What type of investment is good for me at this point in my life?
2. Will I stand to lose money if the market becomes volatile?
3. What type of return can I expect to see on this investment, short and long term?

I would suggest that before you decide to invest your money, you research your options. It is important that while investing, you consider two main ideas, retirement and emergencies. When thinking of retirement, estimate when you want to retire, and calculate how much you can afford to save monthly in your life now, to set you up comfortably then. The second idea to consider is do you have money saved in case of emergency? Events happen in life that you did not see coming or may not have control over, such as losing your job, or accidents and emergencies. Try and save money for these occurrences. When doing so you want to invest in something that has no possibility of depreciating, past your initial investment.

Some key things to be aware of: long term means you can be aggressive, as there is time for the amount of money to rise and fall with the market. Aggressive investments can result in you losing money but they have the highest return. If you see your investment losing money, it is nothing to worry about as you have years before retirement and it can come back. However, it is good practice to have yearly investment checkups, to make sure you are not losing more than you will be able to recover. When investing short-term you do not want to see a loss, as there is more of a possibility of you using that money for short term amenities, like your house, car, or emergencies.

I am not an expert, however I do know it is important to invest your money and set yourself up for the future. Think long-term about where you want to be and what you want to be able to do when you retire. Research and talk to people who are professionals in the financial field and get them to make your retirement thoughts a reality.

Invest your money.

Nick

NEVER LOSE SIGHT OF YOUR GOALS

"In life you are either growing or you are dying." — Lou Holtz

Dear brother,

You need to set goals in your life. If you don't have a direction, you will wonder at all that's passed you by when you wake up middle aged, with no sense of accomplishment. Your goals do not have to be lofty, world or life changing. Not everybody is a Craig Keilburger or a Stephen Lewis. However, setting goals in your life is not only important, in my opinion it is a necessity.

Everyone needs a direction. The key to setting goals is to start off with small, easily attainable goals that you can build confidence with. As you reach the goals you set, you will start to feel good about yourself and before long, you actually start setting goals that are more and more involved. In time, this will garner the confidence you need to do anything.

It does not matter what you are doing. If you think you can accomplish something, you can. Something that worked for me, while setting goals is writing them down. I put them into three categories: weekly, monthly and yearly. Use this template to write your goals if you like.

Weekly	Monthly	Yearly
1.	1.	1.
2.	2.	2.
3.	3.	3.

I found that prioritizing my goals made it easier for me to keep them straight. If, by the end of the week, I didn't reach my goal, I carried it over, and I worked extra hard to get that goal accomplished within the next week. The monthly and yearly goals were treated the same way. I used this process as a guideline to keep me on track. This method kept me focused and motivated and before I knew it, I was starting to cross items off the list more often than not.

Goal setting in life is important. Find goals that you can accomplish and set out to achieve them. We are on this earth for a short period of time, so take advantage of it. Accomplish everything you can. If you set your mind and heart to something, there is nothing that you cannot accomplish. If success through goal setting can be rewarding for others, then it will work for you as well. Set goals, and set yourself up for success.

Never lose sight of your goals.

Nick

THE OPPOSITE OF COURAGE IS NOT JUST COWARDICE BUT ALSO CONFORMITY

"Courage is not simply one of the virtues, but the form of every virtue at the testing point." — C.S Lewis

Dear brother,

People often talk about courage and its antithesis being cowardice, and for the most part that's true. Cowardice is listed in the dictionary as the antonym for courage; however, I believe that the opposite of courage is also conformity. Conforming to the masses is easy to do! It does not take as much work, and it is easy to let someone do the thinking for you. It is easy to let another person's actions dictate your own. Any man can follow the crowd. Be your own man even if it's hard; do not follow the norm because it is easy.

I remember being in high school and making fun of the boys and girls, who chose to be different from the crowd. I teased the young people, who didn't care what the majority thought because they knew the importance of individualism. I know now that I teased them because I admired them. I guess you could say, I was jealous of them for having the courage to wear what they wanted, and to act the way they wanted. I was mad at myself because I conformed to what my group was. I even stayed away from some of the things that I was interested in because at the time, I thought it may not have been perceived as acceptable with my friends.

I remember it was not until I was in university that I began to write, read and be creative for pleasure. I started to explore other interests because I was finally confident enough to do so. I found that while doing so, my perception of the world changed. I started looking at issues and points of view more subjectively, listening and trying to understand the different ideologies of others, rather than just stating my own. As I was doing so a funny thing happened, my friends, who I thought would make fun of me, were the ones who were the most accepting. They embraced my differences, which in turn gave me the confidence to explore other realms.

Life is way too short not to do the things that interest you. I am by no means saying that getting married, having kids and a dog, buying a house and living in the city is conforming. If that is what interests you, I say go for it. What I am saying is do the things that make you happy. If your friends like football and you like art, then like art. Throw your hat in the ring when it comes to trying new things. The people who have courage are the people who will go after the things that make them happy, despite what the majority say or think about it. I read a quote by Theodore Roosevelt that helps emphasize my point, it went as follows:

> *It is not the critic who counts, not the man who points out how the strong man stumbles or where the doer of deeds could have done them better. The credit belongs to the man who is actually in the arena, whose face is marred by dust and sweat and blood, who strives valiantly, who errs and comes short again and again because there is no effort without error and shortcomings, who knows the great devotion, who spends himself in a worthy cause, who at best knows in the end the high achievement of triumph and who at worst, if he fails while daring greatly, knows his place shall never be with those timid and cold souls who know neither victory nor defeat.*
>
> *Theodore Roosevelt*

The opposite of courage is not just cowardice, but also conformity.

Nick

SEIZE THE OPPORTUNITY

"Opportunity is missed by most people because it is dressed in overalls and looks like work." — Thomas Edison

Dear brother,

Opportunities will present themselves in many forms. During your life you will be faced with many situations, in which an opportunity will disguise itself. When that happens it is up to you to decide if it is worth going after. It may not be something as clear as what you see in the movies, or read in books, as opportunities often do not present themselves so definitively. It is common to have to work to obtain opportunities. I have found in my life, the people who have had the most opportunity and success are the ones who worked the hardest to get them.

Do not live with the regret of not going after what is presented to you in life. Not very long ago, I had a wonderful opportunity to entertain a crowd at the historic Empire Theatre in Belleville, Ontario. For a long time, I had wanted to entertain people in the form of stand-up comedy. I have been writing comedy for years but never shared my material with anyone. Finally, I decided the time was now and made a few phone calls to some local celebrities, who were promoting and producing the show. After some convincing, they agreed to give me the opportunity. As the show grew closer, I grew more and more apprehensive, thinking what if I fail? Then a funny thing happened, I started to look at the positive side of pulling this off. I thought to myself, I belong on stage and I can do this. I started to think about how I would feel after it was all done. I convinced myself that I had worked too hard to fail and that I would be successful.

When the time came, I prepared and went on stage in front of over seven hundred people and performed. I am so grateful that I took advantage of the opportunity; it was one of the most rewarding of my life. You are going to be faced with many opportunities as you grow older, so do what you can to make the best of as many as possible. It is not what we do in life that we regret, it's the things we don't do.

Seize the opportunity.

Nick

GOOD THOUGHT BRINGS GOOD THINGS

"Once you replace negative thoughts with positive ones you will
start having positive results."
— Willie Nelson

Dear brother,

You might be thinking that this is going to be a pep talk, echoing every positive thinking book on the shelf. There are some fantastic reads out there that try and educate people on positive thought and how thinking you have something, will get you anything you want. I am not pontificating from any of these, as I said when I started writing these letters, everything I speak about is from personal experience or from something that I have seen in my lifetime. That said, I do have to share a story that emphasizes the fact that if you think about getting things, you can get them.

In "Seize the Opportunity," I spoke of an opportunity that I had to perform at the Empire Theatre. What I didn't speak about was that I set that as a goal for myself a year earlier. I was at the Empire Theatre with my girlfriend watching a variety show. Without really thinking about it, I leaned over to her and said, "Next year, I am going to be performing in this show." She was probably thinking to herself, how? As far as she knew, I was not particularly talented in any of the arts.

All I know is I thought of that show for a year and somehow the universe, happenstance, or being at the right place at the right time made it a reality. A year to the day from my decision, I was performing at the show as a comedian. I am telling you this because thinking about something worked for me. I know because it really happened for me. I also know I am going to start setting more goals and thinking about them, in order for more opportunities to occur in my life.

Good thought brings good things.

Nick

Always be Professional

"Professionalism is knowing how to do it,
when to do it, and doing it."
— Frank Tyger

Dear brother,

Being a professional at work is important. It is important to handle yourself with class, dignity and with an aura that is a cut above most. Be friendly and courteous to colleagues. You do not have to be friends with the people you work with, but you should be as helpful and as gracious to people as you can. You will spend a lot of time at work, so get to know the people who work alongside you. If you are lucky enough to find, a friend or a few friends, that is good thing.

Be a team player. If someone asks for your assistance on something, do not hesitate to lend a hand or offer some advice if asked. You need to know your job, whatever it is. The more you know about the position you are holding, the more valuable you are going to be to the company you work for. Educate yourself at work. Take the programs offered and enhance your credentials.

Take initiative. Do not wait to be asked by a colleague or your superior to do something. If you have a feeling something needs to get done, then do it. I am not telling you to do other people's jobs or to undermine your colleagues. Work within the team concept but take the initiative, look at the big picture and think to yourself, how can I benefit this organization? Find an answer, and then act on it.

Always be professional.

Nick

Always Enter a Room with Confidence and Your Head Up

"Be the man you know that you are."
– Unknown Author

Dear brother,

It is important to enter a room with confidence and with your head up. Look people in the eye when you walk into a room. It shows presence. Stand up tall and be comfortable. It does not matter who you are as far as stature goes. If you have confidence, you will gain the ability to talk to anyone. People are people, we all want to be liked and to be appreciated. The key to being able to talk to anyone is to know what you have to offer to the conversation. Find who you are as a man and be comfortable with that.

I heard a story the other day from a comedian. He was talking about his life, how he is from a small town, where many of the guys he hangs out with always bug him because he is not interested in the same things they are. One night, they were drinking in the barn and one of his buddies asked him to bench press a hundred pounds on the weight set. After a few minutes of banter and taunting, the comedian spoke up and said "Give it a rest man. I can't bench press that much weight and I will never be able to. However, I can find the verb in a sentence."

That shut his buddy up. But what I took from that story is you don't have to be "into" everything your friends are into. Your friends are your friends and they will be forever. Have enough confidence in the person you are, you do not need to be the same as them, in order to fit in.

Having confidence gives you the ability to do anything you put your mind to. Confidence in my opinion is the key to any person's success, it will be the key to yours. Have an edge. If you need help gaining that confidence, look back at all of the things you have accomplished in your life and be proud of them. You are the man that you are because of the experiences you have undergone, through the life you have lived.

Always enter a room with confidence and your head up.

Nick

Work Hard at Whatever You Do

"Hard work spots the light, the character of people.
Some turn up their sleeves, some turn up their noses
and some don't turn up at all."
— Sam Ewing

Dear brother,

Hard work is called hard work because it is hard. I know that sounds like a relatively simple line but if you think about it, it's true. If you work hard at everything you do, you will frequently wind up being satisfied with what you accomplish. I believe there is nothing in this world that cannot be accomplished if a person decides to work at it.

There really is no substitute for working hard, with hard work comes a sense of pride. When you can look back on your day, week, month or year and think to yourself that you have accomplished what you have because you were not afraid to make a sacrifice, you will find gratification.

Think for a moment of the people that you find the most successful, the people that look as though they have the best of everything this world has to offer: the house, the cars, the great job, or a great family, love and a balanced life. Now try and remember the amount of work they put in to obtain these things. With hard work, you can accomplish anything. Every person that I know, that I deem a success, has worked very hard for every cent and amenity they have. They realized in their life, nothing was going to come easy but if they put in the hours at the gym or at the office, they would find their success simply through working hard.

Working hard teaches life lessons. If you don't accomplish immediately what you set out to do, remember that you will always be ahead of the person who decided that they will just take life as it comes and not work or sacrifice to get to where they want to be.

You determine your work ethic. You may not be the most talented or the smartest but you can always work the hardest. All you need is the drive and the will to succeed. I think most people want the amenities of life, but not everyone wants to put forth the effort needed to get them. You will be rewarded if you work hard.

Work hard at everything you do.

Nick

BE JUDGED ON YOUR ACTIONS, NOT YOUR WORDS

"I never worry about action, but only about inaction."
— Winston Churchill

Dear brother,

Actions are far stronger and more effective than words. I believe telling someone how you feel is for you, while showing them how you feel is for them. It is easy to say how much you care for someone, but unless you follow through with actions that are conducive to the words that you use, then my advice is to not use the words at all.

I remember once, I had a crush on a young woman named Jocelyn. We were friends, and I thought that she was such a great person and that we would be good together. However, I messed things up with her romantically before the potential relationship ever had a chance to get started. In short, I went with a woman with whom I had a previous history, for no reason other than it was safe. Needless to say, the "safer" choice did not work out. I was actually fortunate to still be friends with Jocelyn. She was selfless and forgiving and I was happy to be a part of her life.

One night we were walking home together and I expressed to her how much I appreciated her as a friend. I thought that she and I would make a great couple, if she could find it in her heart to give me another chance. I continued with this long, well rehearsed speech, outlining what it was I could bring to the relationship if given the opportunity.

I was certainly not prepared for what she said next. I had visions of her leaping into my arms and the two of us riding off into the metaphorical sunset together, she had different ideas. She told me that, sincerity in words means very little without action. I had done nothing to show her in the last days, weeks, or months that I meant any of the things I said to her. She continued, "Words are for you and without actions, they are empty." I would have loved to have seen my face when she told me that, as you know I am a man of many words and in a few short sentences, I was rendered speechless.

Shortly after we parted ways to go home, I knew what she had said was right. Everything that she told me made sense and from that moment, I made changes in my life. I vowed I would never tell anyone how I felt, unless I was prepared to show them. It may not have worked out between my friend and I, however, I will always be grateful for the important life lesson she taught me. How you feel only affects yourself. Actions are what affect other people. Words without actions are empty, so be a man of action.

Be judged on your actions, not your words.

Nick

Walk Like You Know Something Others Don't

"Go where there is no path and leave a trail."
– Ralph Waldo Emerson

Dear brother,

Do not under any circumstances, let anyone tell you how to act. In life you will get advice from people you respect and love. Listen to them, as they are the important people in your life. Conversely, you will also be given advice from people that you hardly know. Under no circumstances do I want you to conform to what they have to say. You are your own man and you act the way you do because of your individualism and uniqueness. Do not act the way people tell you to just because their ideas are deemed the norm.

When I was in grade nine, just fourteen years old, I walked around with confidence. I did not for one minute think I was better than anyone but I was a confident, young kid. To some people that came across as being cocky and because of the way I acted, sometimes people would take exception and target me. I remember being told by one of my friends, if I didn't change the way I walked around school, I was going to get my butt kicked by some of the older boys. I had no idea why. I thought to myself, they don't even know me, why would they want to hurt me because of the way I walked?

I remember going home that night and being confused as to what I needed to do. I called our cousin Brandon, who was away at University and asked him what I should do. He told me that the problem was not mine, it was theirs. My initial thought was, yeah well it is going to be my problem when they stuff me inside a locker. However, he continued to talk and told me that "They were picking on me, because they did not like my confidence, I was a young guy with a bit of swagger and not everyone liked that, but at least at the end of the day I would know that I was who I was because I believed in myself."

When I hung up the phone, I realized he was right. I went to school the next day and nothing happened. I knew my friends liked me and that was good enough. I stayed true to who I was; I didn't change my walk or the way I acted. A funny thing happened: those older guys never picked a fight with me. In fact, after they were able to get to know me a little bit, some became my friends. The truth is, you are who you are. Your friends and family will always be there because they love the person you are, no matter who you choose to be. Changes in life will occur, but promise yourself that you will never change the person you are for fear of not fitting in. You are you, and that is good enough.

Walk like you know something others don't.

Nick

You Won't Ever Fail if You Don't Ever Give Up!

"You are not going to win every day in sport. You are not going to win every day in life. But the difference between winners and losers in sport and in life is how you react after defeat."
— Tony Dungy

Dear brother,

Failure in life never has to be an option. If you never stop trying, no one will be able to fail you. I've always believed that, just because you did not pass, it does not have to mean you have failed. I firmly believe a person will only fail at something, if they give up trying. If you don't pass a driving test the first time, are you going to go through your life not ever wanting to drive? Chances are you will retake the test, and you will be awarded the convenience of driving.

I played hockey with a guy who was cut from his junior team. However, upon receiving the news, he refused to leave. He actually stayed in his car for two days, parked at the rink. He sat in the stands at practice, hoping to convince the coach to give him another chance. The coach refused but he stayed anyway. One day there was an injury and the team couldn't call anyone up to play. They gave him his second opportunity. He played and not only did he end up making the team, but he was later drafted to the NHL and played professionally. If this young man had quit on his dream to be a hockey player, he would have failed. He didn't, and through determination and persistence, he found a way to be successful.

Strive for success and understand that success is measured by your own terms. It is important not to judge yourself, on other people's pretences or their accomplishments. You should be your own measuring stick. Set a goal and do what you can to accomplish it. It is important to understand that you can use your failures as steps toward your success. You may not be successful the first time you attempt to accomplish something, however, use the experience that you have gained through trying, as a step toward becoming a success.

Act as though it is impossible to fail when you are living your life. Have confidence in the person you are, but do not walk around thinking you are better than anybody. People, who act like that, do not garner respect and are regarded as pompous. Be confident in you and live your life to a standard, which sets certain men apart. If you act as though it is impossible to fail, you will not.

You won't ever fail, if you don't ever give up.

Nick

PART TWO

RESPECT

Don't Drink and Drive

"It takes 8,460 bolts to assemble an automobile and one nut to scatter it all over the road."
— Author Unknown (Bumper Sticker)

Dear brother,

It is simple, if there is anything in this world I want you to remember, it is **DON'T DRINK AND DRIVE!** Please. I can give you examples and statistics of people who died, killed somebody, ruined their life or went to jail, when they decided to get behind the wheel after drinking. However, I do not need to. To understand what can happen to you when you drink and drive, read the letter: 'You will always have a choice.' "A small" part of this letter reads; "Life up to that point had not prepared me for that news, I did not know what to do. I walked to the basement of the house, so as not to wake any of my roommates and I called my dad." I encourage you to read the rest.

The number of people that think they can risk driving because they view themselves as indestructible is staggering. I was young once too, I know how easy it is to be influenced to drive while drunk. If you ever have any doubt call me, a cab, a friend, anyone, just do not drive drunk.

Don't drink and drive.

Nick

If You Have Something to Say to Someone Say it

"The difference between a smart man and a wise man is that a
smart man knows what to say,
a wise man knows whether or not to say it."
— Frank M. Garafola

Dear brother,

One of the biggest problems many are faced with is that they bottle things up. Even if it isn't bothersome, just something you deem important, then get it off your chest. It may, in some cases be difficult to say, however, I know from experience that if you are carrying something inside you and it is weighing on you, then say it. Holding it in will do more harm than good.

In school not too long ago, I dated a woman, who I really liked. We really enjoyed each other's company. She had every characteristic I wanted in a woman. The problem was I just did not know how to express myself. I waited and waited for the day to come, to say to her how I really felt. Unfortunately, that day never came and we both knew it was not going to come, even though I wanted so badly to have the courage to articulate how I was feeling. My time to say how I was feeling had come and gone without me knowing it, eventually we lost touch. However, I realized that she was always in my heart, memories of our time together were a consistent fixture in my mind. One day, years later, I called and she agreed to meet me for a coffee. When I saw her, the emotions I had felt came back. We talked and caught up on the happenings of each other's life.

When the day ended I hugged her and went to my car, where I sat for a few minutes. Not wanting to let another possibility to express what I had been harboring for so long slip by, I got out and knocked on her door. She answered, and when she saw me standing there, I could tell by the look on her face she was surprised. I asked if I could have a few to minutes tell her something that had been on my mind and she said yes. So I began. I told her what I was about to say came from the heart, and without agenda. I continued to tell her that without knowing it, she had left more of an impression on me than anyone in my life, for that I would be forever greatful. I wanted her to appreciate I loved her unconditionally and wished her nothing but happiness.

I was not asking for a response or for anything in return. When I finished what I wanted to say, I turned and left. Telling her how I felt gave me the capacity to move forward, it lifted the burden of bottling something up, which should have been released years ago. As for the girl to whom the message was told, my hope is that the expression of how I felt made her a little happier.

If you have something to say to someone say it.

Nick

KNOW WHEN TO INTRODUCE YOURSELF

"Always give a word or sign of salute when meeting or passing a
friend, or even a stranger, if in a lonely place."
— Tecumseh

Dear brother,

You need to know when it is the right time to introduce yourself. I distinctly remember being in University and my friend
Danielle called me to meet her and some of her colleagues for a
drink. I agreed and went to the bar to meet her. Immediately we
struck up a conversation. After a few minutes my friend went to
the other end of the establishment to get a couple beers. No big
deal, except for the fact that while we were talking, it had slipped
her mind to introduce me to her friends. This left me sitting at the
table, in a vagarious position nodding my head and smiling, looking
for commonality with complete strangers. It was not until sometime
later that the guy sitting across from me introduced himself, which
finally broke the ice.

I am not sure if there is proper etiquette as to when you are sup-
posed to introduce yourself. If there is not, there should be. I suggest that if you have not been introduced immediately, then do it
within thirty to forty five seconds of your arrival. It makes it less
awkward if you are forced to fend for yourself.

When I was in university our cousin Kathy and I had a system.
If we were out together and someone came up to me and I did not
introduce her, then right away she knew it was because I didn't remember their name. Our system was that she would then introduce
herself, prompting the person to reciprocate the gesture by intro-

ducing themselves and hopefully using their name. I would pick up on the using of the person's name, then use the name to complete the introduction back to them. Confused? It would sound like this:

Stranger: "Hi Nick, how are you?"

Me: "Hey bud! How are you? How long has it been? Seems like ages!"

Cousin: "Hi! I am Nick's cousin, Kathy?"

Stranger: "Hi Kathy, I am James."

Me: "Oh, where is my head? James - Kathy, Kathy - James.

See? Foolproof, unless of course the person does not use their name, then good luck. If they do, the person is not any wiser, and you do not look like a fool for forgetting the name of someone who has not forgotten yours.

Know when to introduce yourself.

Nick

LIVE WITH CHIVALRY

"Some say that the age of chivalry is past, that the spirit of romance is dead. The age of chivalry is never past so long as there is a wrong left undressed on earth."
— Charles Kingsley

Dear brother,

Let chivalry be a part of your life, always. I have found that throughout my life the most rewarding moments I have experienced are those that I have helped a friend, colleague or stranger in a time of need. Wherever possible, lend your support or services to someone and after doing so, do not expect any favour in return.

Not very long ago, I was working as a teacher in England. I remember one afternoon, I was taking a group of young people into London for the day, as a class trip. These young people were from a group home that I worked in. So, without divulging too much of the backgrounds of these students, you should understand that they certainly did not grow up privy to the same family structure that we are accustomed to.

As the six of us, (my four students, me and my teaching assistant) were sitting on the train talking about the events that were planned for the day, four women got on at a stop. The kids were sitting in a group of seats beside my colleague and I. Before I could offer up my seat to one of the women, all of my students at the same time got up and gave them their seat. I couldn't believe it! The women were thrilled, and gladly took them up on the offer. My students stood for the entire thirty-minute train journey to London. What I found interesting was that the women, as they sat beside me, had no idea that they were my students. As they began to speak amongst themselves, I heard one woman say something that I will never forget: "It is so nice to see, chivalry isn't dead."

I was so proud of my students. They saw it as a small gesture of respect, I saw it as a huge step towards spreading small acts of good in a world that can certainly use it. I have no idea where those young boys and girls are, or what they are doing now. I am also certain in my years of teaching, I have taught students that have become more successful. I can also say, without reservation, that I have never been more proud of a group.

Live with chivalry.

Nick

RESPECT A MAN OR WOMAN IN UNIFORM

"Twenty-five million veterans are living among us today. These men and women selflessly set aside their civilian lives to put on the uniform and serve us."
— Steve Buyer

Dear brother,

You need to always respect people who are in uniform. Whether it is mall security or a decorated military person, the reality is they've earned the uniform and we should respect them because of it. I have heard many times in my life that freedom is not free, that has always resonated with me. Our autonomy continues to be protected by young men and women who risk their lives every day, in countries that we may have never seen or heard of, to keep our freedom.

On September 11th police, firefighters, medics and soldiers risked and gave their lives without hesitation, in order to save the lives of others. That is the highest form of bravery I can think of. I believe it is a testament to all that is good in the world, that everyone came together and did what they could to help the citizens of New York and Washington. The fact that so much good came from such evil is a tribute to humanity.

The job of keeping the peace or saving lives can be tiresome and thankless, if not for these brave men and women our world would not be the way we know it. The privileges we have grown accustomed to over the years, have been received, due to the people who have dedicated their lives to our safety. They have earned our respect, so give it to them…always.

Respect a man or woman in uniform.

Nick

STAY SOBER ON YOUR WEDDING DAY

"Always do sober what you said you'd you do drunk. That will
teach you to keep your mouth shut."
— Ernest Hemmingway

Dear brother,

There is nothing tackier than a drunken, babbling, idiot groom. In my life I have been able to attend many weddings, some I have even had the privilege of being a part of. I have to say the weddings I attended, where the groom or the groomsmen were walking around incoherently drunk, seemed to be the worst experiences.

The day is not about you. I know that you have to be there in order to make it happen, and it is indeed a memory that you should always cherish. However, not very often when growing up into adulthood are you going to be dreaming about the day you get married. Your partner on the other hand may have had the dream wedding all planned out; you do not want to leave her with a memory of you passing out at the receiving table, the victim of a round of boiler makers with the groomsmen.

If you happen to be a groomsman, remember you were invited there as a supporting member of the wedding. You are there to complement the couple, not to be the talk of the town the next day, so act accordingly. As a groomsman, if you are asked to make a speech, take the honour seriously. Do not drink so much liquid courage; you end up in front of everyone rambling on about nothing. If you are not a talker keep it short. If you have to drink, stay sober long enough to at least deliver your speech. The couple will appreciate the gesture.

If you are the groom remember to pay close attention to your bride. More than likely, she has put in an endless amount of work trying to get everything perfect or as close to perfect as she can. This means that you will need to reassure her on how great everything has turned out, how amazing she looks and how lucky you are to have her. You should not need to be reminded to do this: she is your bride! It should come naturally, just do not forget. The reality is the jobs you will be given will be minute, due to her fear of you screwing them up. Do what you are asked with a smile, and be there for her to lean on if needed.

My friend Paul got married during the potential threat of a hurricane, which meant that there was going to be a last minute venue change. The bride, Ashley handled it like a star, rolling with the punches and doing what needed to be done. My friend, the groom, was there to support her every decision, and as a result the wedding turned out beautifully.

Finally, please arrive on time. The bride can be late, yes, but you cannot, no excuses.

Stay sober on your wedding day.

Nick

Courtesy Gets You Everywhere

"Life is not so short but that there is always time for courtesy."
— Ralph Waldo Emerson

Dear brother,

I remember asking my boss, what I should do when I feel that a person I am trying to help is not showing me any respect. His response? "Kill them with kindness." He explained to me that it is important to be courteous to everyone you meet. It does not mean you have to be a push-over or someone that is taken advantage of. You do not have to shower everyone you meet with gifts or compliments. Simply be a nice person. It does not take any effort to smile, or to listen to someone and respond with kindness.

Being courteous to people will make you feel better about yourself. Life is sometimes going to present you with circumstances, where people will not like the predicament they are in and as a result, they take it out on you. If that is the case, I ask you to be friendly. Do not add fuel to the fire with defensive remarks, which will do nothing but compound negativity. Chances are you may not be aware what this person has been through, to make them act in this manner.

Be the first to hold the door for someone or to say hello. Be the first to help out, or offer your hand for assistance. Be the first to show compassion and offer a kind gesture. Be the first to say thank you; be the first to offer a compliment. Be the first to be courteous to others, no matter the time or place.

Courtesy gets you everywhere.

Nick

Firm Handshakes are Important

"Look him right in his eyes, the man may know a lot about you
by your handshake."
— Clint Eastwood-Gran Torino

Dear brother,

It is important that when you shake hands with someone, you have a firm grip. A firm handshake shows that you have confidence. When meeting someone for business or for pleasure, or as a gesture to a friend, make sure your hand shake has some substance behind it. There is nothing worse than shaking hands with a person and they have a dead-fish, limp hand shake, the kind of shake that is just out there with no grip or substance. Immediately that person comes across as someone who does not have confidence.

When are firm handshakes important? Firm handshakes are always important but especially under the following circumstances.

1. Prospective employers: you want to be able to show your employer you are confident and are ready for what the job will entail.
2. Meeting parents of your partner: most fathers you meet are judging your every move so make sure that when you shake the hand of the father, have a grip and don't be shy. Give it a little extra squeeze just to let him know you are there.
3. A job well done: A good job should always be solidified with a firm handshake or to confirm to someone they have done a job well.
4. Cementing a deal or a sale: shaking hands after a purchase or a

sale gives the transaction closure.

5. After receiving advice: financial, social, or emotional- it does not matter. Shaking hands shows that you are appreciative.

There are many situations when a handshake is important. Whenever you shake hands, do it with confidence and as a man who sees himself as an equal to the person with whom he is shaking hands. Do not be meek, be strong with your grip and shake hands with conviction.

Firm handshakes are important.

Nick

LOOK A PERSON IN THE EYE WHEN SPEAKING TO THEM

"I have looked into your eyes with my eyes.
I have put my heart with your heart."
— Pope John XXIII

Dear brother,

It may not be the easiest thing to do but when you are speaking to someone, look them in the eye. Doing so is a sign of respect. It shows the person you are speaking with that they have your full attention. Some may find it awkward to look someone in the eye when speaking. I suggest you do your best to practice it when you can, making eye contact from time to time shows that you are engaged in the conversation. In my experience, it demonstrates you are taking the conversation seriously and your thoughts are not elsewhere.

I remember being in a conversation with a gentlemen and he would not even glance at me when we were speaking. I really did not know what to think. I was not sure if I had his attention. I found myself trying to look at the things that he was looking at. Needless to say, the conversation did not last very long, as we both lost interest. Either that or we forgot what we were talking about.

Look a person in the eye when speaking to them.

Nick

Never Start Eating Your Dinner
before the Rest of the Table

"Good manners sometimes means simply putting up with other
peoples bad manners."
– H Jackson Brown Jr.

Dear brother,

I remember when I was a rookie playing junior hockey, I was
waiting for my dinner at a restaurant with the rest of my team, and
my dinner happened to get to me before the rest of the table. Not
knowing the etiquette, I began to eat my dinner. I didn't get my
first bite of pasta to my mouth before a veteran stopped me and not
so kindly reminded me that rookies did not eat, or did anything for
that matter, before the veterans.

Being told by my veteran teammate not to eat my dinner before
the rest of the table got me thinking. It really is not a respectable
practice to eat before everyone has received their plate. If you consider it, it makes sense, and really it is just a common courtesy that
should be extended to anyone you are dining with. It is not very
polite to force the rest of the table to watch while you enjoy your
meal. It is simple: get your meal and wait. Once you have seen
everyone has received their plate, then it is safe to proceed with
yours.

Never start eating your dinner before the rest of the table.

Nick

ONLY MAKE THE FIRST MOVE WHEN INVITED

"Courtesy is as much a mark of a gentleman as courage."
— Theodore Rosevelt

Dear brother,

Dating can be difficult, and the only thing I can say for certain is that I am no expert. When going on dates there are things you cannot control. These are the situations that are out of your hands, like chemistry, commonality and attraction. In my opinion, they are either there or they are not. If they are - great but if they are not, there is nothing you can do to make it happen. I know from experience, it is impossible to force a connection with someone.

If however, there is a connection, then as a man, you need to remember while on a date always be a gentleman. If things are going well and you feel your date wants you to kiss her, then you need to be prepared to look for the signs. First - kisses can be complicated, maybe not in the semantics of the kiss, but when it comes to reading the signs. Women will let you know whether or not they want to be kissed. Here are some of the signs I have noticed over the years that are sure-fire ways to tell if a woman wants you to kiss her.

1. At the end of the night when you walk your date to the door, they are looking you in the eye and smiling and when you lean in for a kiss, they reciprocate the gesture.
2. They are attentive the whole date and are consistently making touching gestures, such as her hand on yours, her hand on your back, her foot on your foot, and other consistent light touches

through the night.

3. When they lean forward and are looking at you, they want you to kiss them.
4. Look into her eyes. If a woman wants to be kissed, you can see it in their eyes.

You need to understand the signs and follow them. You should be able to feel, if giving your date a kiss is the right thing. If the signs are not there, and you are not feeling them, chances are she is not feeling them either. Do not try and create the spark by giving a kiss, in most cases it does not work that way for women. They have to be into it before they go through with it. Make sure you are cognizant of that.

Only make the first move when invited.

Nick

Stay Balanced

"Life is like riding a bicycle. To keep your balance you must
keep moving."
— Albert Einstein

Dear brother,

You need to live a healthy and balanced life if you want to be healthy into old age. I know as young people, we often have delusions of being invincible, we sometimes neglect taking care of our bodies because we feel as though we are going to be young forever. When keeping your body balanced, remember, staying balanced consists of three things: Mind, Body and Spirit.

Keep your mind healthy. This can be done by using a plethora of activities: It can be anything from mind benders on handheld devices, to reading or writing. You need to keep an active mind. Challenge yourself to do things which are out of your comfort zone and make you think. Going to work and following the same routine everyday is not going to keep your mind sharp. Look for things that interest you and keep a sharp mind by doing them.

Exercise your body. I know it is far easier to say than to do, and as we get older it gets more and more difficult to drag yourself to the gym, with the weight of everyday life commitments hindering the process. However, if you cannot get to the gym every day, then I suggest doing activities such as gardening, walking, and playing in recreational leagues. A minimum of twenty minutes a day is what you should strive for although sixty is better. Keep active as you get older, you will be happy you did.

Be spiritual. Immediately people think, by being spiritual you need to be religious, but that is not the case. If religion brings you happiness, you should worship whenever you feel it is necessary. However, to me being spiritual means being in touch with yourself as an individual. Having spirituality in your life is opening yourself to new possibilities, learning from other cultures, and applying what you have learned to your own life. Spirituality is for you and you alone. Get in touch with your spiritual side by doing something that will help you maintain your overall well-being.

Stay balanced.

Nick

PART THREE

LOVE & FAMILY

ALWAYS BRING SOMETHING ON A FIRST DATE

"If you think there are no frontiers, watch a boy ring the front
doorbell on his first date."
— Olin Miller

Dear brother,

I went on this date the other night and everything that could
have gone wrong did. First of all, the date we originally planned
for did not work for either of us, so we had to reschedule twice.
When we agreed on a date and met, we found out at the restaurant
that I had made reservations, an hour later than we thought. By the
time we received our menus, it was time to meet our friends at the
bar, so we couldn't eat. The bar was a dive and the drinks were
served in plastic cups, as apparently people had a habit of getting
drunk and throwing empty glasses across the establishment. Needless to say, we did not have much going for us that night.

To make a long story short, we actually turned the night around
with some good conversation, drinks and my amazing dance
moves! (Yes, you can stop laughing now). Anyway, as I was walking her back to her place, I asked what she thought was the best
part of the night. Her reply, she thought it was cute that I brought
her a gift. She told me she'd never had anyone bring her anything
on a first date, and thought it was very considerate.

I am no Casanova, trust me, I have had my fair share of disaster
dates, but the one thing that I will always remember to do is bring
something on a first date. It does not have to be something you
bought, or anything that is expensive. A small gift shows that you
are a gentleman and took the time to think of her. I am not going to

tell you what you should bring, that's the point. Get an understanding of who they are, what they will appreciate and make the gesture.

Always bring something on a first date.

Nick

Always Walk On the Outside, Closest To the Road

"As people are walking all the time,
in the same spot, a path appears."
— John Locke

Dear brother,

When walking with a woman or a child, I want you to always make sure to walk on the part of the sidewalk that is closest to the road. This was common practice many years ago, as men walked closer to the road to protect the women from the splash of horse and buggy, as well as from danger. I fear this small gesture has been lost on men over the decades.

It is very simple to do. Every time you are walking with a women or a child, position yourself so that you are closer to traffic. At first, the person you are walking with may wonder what you are doing, as you are always moving and manipulating yourself between them and traffic. If they ask, you can tell them your reasoning, however, more often than not you will just get a funny look. Women of course, are capable of looking after themselves, yet I believe that most want to be protected. This small gesture is a nice way of showing them you think of their well-being, as well as their safety.

Always walk on the outside, closest to the road.

Nick

Be Good To Mom

"There's nothing like a mama-hug."
— Terri Guillemets

Dear brother,

I once heard being a mother is the most difficult, yet rewarding job there is. I can say unequivocally that we have the best. Mom has been there for our family since the beginning, and we are blessed to have her. Make sure that you always treat her with the respect and love she deserves. She has been a pillar in our lives, the cornerstone of our family, sacrificing so much to help us succeed, supporting our athletics, helping us with our homework, being there for us to lean on, lending her ear to listen, offering advice… doing everything and anything to help us become good people.

I remember a time at a young age, when mom was up getting me ready to go to a hockey tournament, with an older group of boys. She could tell I was nervous because I did not know what to expect. When my ride arrived and I was walking out the door, she stopped me, gave me kiss and said, "The cream always rises to the top son, you will do great." I am not sure if that gesture was due to a mother's intuition, but it was something that instantly made me feel better and I have never forgot. Mom knows who we are as people and over the years, she has given us the tools to be successful.

A friend once told me they can tell if a man is going to be good to his wife, by the way he treats his mom. If he treats his mom with respect, then he will treat his partner with respect. So be good to her always, as her love for us has always been infinite.

Be good to mom.

Nick

LIVE WITH INTEGRITY, CONVICTION, STRENGTH AND COURAGE

"Integrity is doing the right thing,
even when nobody is watching."
— Unknown Author

Dear brother,

I know life can be difficult, sometimes it is hard to stay on track and stay true to your values. I believe if you follow the virtues of integrity, conviction, strength, and courage you will find that your life will be lived with meaning and purpose.

Having integrity means you live your life with strong moral character; you do the right thing even when it is not the norm. Men that have integrity are the kind of men who are successful in all facets of life, they know the difference between what is right and what is wrong. In my life, I have made many mistakes that have compromised this value, however, I believe I have learned from those mistakes, and more often than not I try to live my life with integrity.

Having conviction in your life means you have a firm belief about something. It is important to have strong convictions, as this makes you accountable. Sitting on the fence will not help you live with conviction. Find something you are passionate about and believe in it: live with conviction.

Strength can be described as having a strong will or moral power. Have the strength to stand up for what you believe in, to answer the critics no matter how hard the question. Be strong in your determination to succeed and do not waiver, when it comes to your moral character. Have the strength to do the right thing.

Finally, have the courage to live without fear. Have the courage to do the things in life that make you happy, the things that challenge you. Life is short, so find the courage to go after your dreams and aspirations. Never let someone tell you that you cannot do it. You can do anything you set your mind to, you just need the courage to get started.

Live with integrity, conviction, strength and courage.

Nick

LOVE YOUR PARTNER'S IMPERFECTIONS

"There is a kind of beauty in imperfection."
— Unknown Author

Dear brother,

Perfection is defined as something that is flawless. What we as men need to understand is everyone has flaws. It is when you learn to love or accept those flaws that you start to see someone for who they are, and love them for that same reason.

Growing up I would often look for reasons to not allow a relationship to work. I would come up with lame excuses to sabotage the whole thing. Excuses like: she walked funny, she snorted when she laughed, we don't listen to the same music, she is a liberal, she is a conservative, she supports the Green Party, or she farts in her sleep... I would use one ridiculous excuse after another to keep every relationship at arm's length.

It was not until I realized I had my own imperfections (which I should have realized long before I did), that I began to accept people for who they were, and appreciate them for all their little imperfections and idiosyncrasies. When I did that, I opened my heart to the possibility of love and was able to find it.

Love your partner's imperfections.

Nick

NEVER GO TO BED ANGRY

"Anger dwells only in the bosom of fools."
— Albert Einstein

Dear brother,

Do not go to bed angry; this may be easier to say than it is to do. I know personally I have not always practiced this, as I have on many occasions gone to bed angry. My advice is to do the best you can to avoid doing this. Do not let things get to a boiling point, where you will refuse to let it go. I am not saying you have to resolve every situation before you go to bed, as sometimes it is important or even helpful, to take a step back from the issue before deciding how you are going to handle it. But if you do so, avoid letting hate and anger be the driving force. Communicate your issue and listen to your partner, so you will arm yourself with both sides of the argument before sleeping on it.

When I was in university, I used to fight with my girlfriend constantly. We were like cats and dogs, like oil and water. We would say malicious things to each other, then go our separate ways, leaving each other to deal with all the hurtful things, which had been said. We would sometimes leave it for too long, letting the fight consume our thoughts and lives. When we decided we were ready to talk, the anger was often still there. It would take time to let the argument go. I could turn one argument into a seven day standoff because of stubbornness. Do not let things get to the point where the issues cannot be resolved. You are not going to agree with everything people say or believe, but remember, life is too short to hold grudges.

Never go to bed angry.

Nick

OPEN THE CAR DOOR FOR A WOMAN

"I would rather trust a woman's instinct than a man's reason."
— Stanley Baldwin

Dear brother,

I understand that opening a car door for a woman is not common practice and sometimes it is not practical to do. However, I will say by opening a door for a woman, it will inherently show them that you respect them. It also shows the woman you are a gentleman.

I remember watching a movie called A Bronx Tale where the lead character opened a door for his date, then walked around the back of the car to see if she reached across to unlock his side. If she did, he would continue courting her, if she did not, he wouldn't. I will never tell you to put any stock in a woman unlocking your side of the car. That said, do your part as a gentleman. The opening of a car door for your date, girlfriend or wife is rarely done these days. It is a practice that may have stopped long before we were born. Be the one to help bring it back! Doing so will make you a bit of an enigma, the mystery man who thinks of little gestures to make his woman smile. At first you may even get a look that says, "What are you doing on this side of the car?" But believe me, the gesture will resonate well. Little things go along way.

Open the car door for a woman.

Nick

OVERSPEND WHEN PURCHASING AN ENGAGEMENT RING

"True love stories never have endings."
— Richard Bach

Dear brother,

As I write this to you, I can honestly say I have no experience when it comes to purchasing an engagement ring. However, I do know (hopefully) you will be lucky enough to only have to do it once. So when making the purchase, I urge you to spend a little more than you can afford. Believe me you will be happy you did. My hope is the woman you buy for will be worth the indulgence. I am not saying break the bank, but if the ring she wants is a little more expensive, then make it happen. I have been told that a happy wife makes for a happy life!

Overspend when purchasing an engagement ring.

Nick

Love like You Have Never Been Hurt

"Sometimes the heart sees what is invisible to the eye."
— H. Jackson Brown

Dear brother,

There will be a time in your life that you will experience heartache, to an extreme that you did not think you were capable of feeling. You may think your world as you know it, is crashing down on you. My advice to you brother is to hold on. It will get easier with time: that I can guarantee you. Take it from a man who has had his heart broken. There is someone out there that will complement you. Hold on to that hope; you will find that love.

When you do find that special someone, that person who makes your heart reverberate, let them in. Do not hold on to the pain and anguish, which you experienced in past relationships. Remember when opening your heart to someone different, they were not the person responsible for your feelings of sadness. I remember meeting Gene, after going through a difficult break up. I did not give her, the attention she deserved because I was still hurting from my previous relationship. I realized it was not fair to treat her in this manner. When I finally opened my mind and heart to the possibilities, I was able to see how she complemented me, and eventually I was able to move forward without trepidation.

Experiencing heartache is part of life. Having scars from the past, means that you were not scared to put yourself out there. Sometimes relationships do not work out, but do not allow stories of failed relationships to keep you from falling in love, with perhaps, the perfect person for you.

Love like you have never been hurt.

Nick

NEVER DISRESPECT YOUR WIFE OR GIRLFRIEND

"Kindness is a language,
which the deaf can hear and the blind can see."
— Mark Twain

Dear brother,

Under no circumstances is there ever a time when it is okay to disrespect your wife or girlfriend. I understand not all days are gems and there are times when arguing your point may seem to be the only option. If you have to argue, I urge you to fight in a fair and calm manner. Do not bring things up, which will be hard for the other person to let go when the argument is over.

You might be thinking, "What types of thing are disrespectful?" I guess the answer to that is when you see the look on your partners face, and it screams "I cannot believe you just said that!" That is a pretty good indication that you have said something disrespectful. Remember, at the end of the day, it is you and your partner that are going to be left side by side. Refrain from making jokes about your partner or their family, in order to make yourself feel good in front of other people. I have seen this happen, where a guy would be with his buddies and he would make jokes at his girlfriend's expense, everyone would be laughing, except of course the girlfriend. I tell you this: you will not be laughing when you get home! Trust me.

There are many things people do to disrespect each other. In order to give you the blanket advice that will cover them all, I want you to remember this: if you are doing something and you wouldn't want your mother or sister treated that way, then chances are you are being disrespectful. Use your head, think things through and stay true to your values. By doing so, you will make more right decisions than wrong.

Never disrespect your wife or girlfriend.

Nick

SHOW YOUR WIFE YOU ARE IN LOVE WITH HER

"My most brilliant achievement was my ability to be able to persuade my wife to marry me."
— Winston Churchill

Dear brother,

As you know I have never been married and I am not sure when that day is going to come. I do however, think it is important to show whoever you marry, you love them in some way, every day. This should not be a chore, your wife will know who she married when she married you, so I am not asking you to do or be anything you are not. I also understand that life can get complicated with time, especially if you add children to the mix.

I want you to understand that showing your wife you love her everyday does not mean breakfast in bed or flowers every morning. There are other things you can do to show your love and gratitude for being in the relationship. The following is a list of simple gestures a man can do for his wife:

1. Take out the garbage, without being asked.
2. Do the dishes without being asked.
3. Cook dinner and have it ready, when she comes home from work.
4. Let her watch whatever program she wants, even when your favorite sporting event is on.
5. Starting her car when it is freezing out!
6. Make her tea or coffee in the morning.
7. Clean the house (including the bathroom.)

8. Take her out on a date during the week.
9. Fold the laundry.
10. Tell her something kind, even when she is in a bad mood.

This list is just to get you started. When the time is right, I am sure you can come up with your own list, as there are many ways to show your wife how much you love her. Remember, I have echoed this to you before, when it comes to love, think action not words.

Show your wife you are in love with her.

Nick

TELL A WOMAN WHO GETS DRESSED UP THAT THEY LOOK BEAUTIFUL

"Be quick to compliment and slow to criticize."
— Dale Carnegie

Dear brother,

It does not take much to pay someone a compliment. I remember a time when I was living in England, my roommate Lauren and I were going to a dinner party with some friends. Our apartment was a busy one, all three of my roommates and I were always going in different directions. On this one particular day, two of our schedules coincided, so we decided that we would get ready at our apartment, have a drink and go to the gathering together. I was waiting for Lauren, when she walked into the room, the first thing that came to my mind was, "Wow you look beautiful!" And without hesitation, I told her those exact words.

She told me I was sweet but the look on her face made my day. I could tell, she was really happy to hear that compliment. That simple gesture made my roommate smile. It didn't cost me anything and took me two seconds to say. The gesture made her feel good about herself, and it also made me feel good about myself. Complimenting people should be something you do every day. You will quickly learn to like the way it makes you and the people around you feel.

Tell a woman who gets dressed up that they look beautiful.

Nick

PART FOUR

PERSONAL MOTIVATIONS & TRUTHS

Tell the Truth

"You will never find yourself until you face the truth."
— Oscar Wilde

Dear brother,

I heard an old adage the other day that said the truth will set you free. Too many times in this world, I have had an opportunity to set myself free by telling the truth but didn't, for fear of having to live with the consequences. As a person who has lied many times in his life, believe me when I tell you, no matter how hard it is, tell the truth.

I remember the day like it was yesterday. I was lying in my bed staring at the ceiling, after a night out with my roommates, when I heard a knock at my bedroom door. When the door opened, my beautiful, long-time, girlfriend was standing in the entrance with a look on her face that I will never forget.

She said, "I am going to ask you this question once, and I want you to answer truthfully because if you don't, you and I will never be able to salvage our relationship." I stared at her for what seemed like an eternity, thinking of a story I could quickly make up, as a rebuttal to whatever it was she was going to say to me. I asked her if everything was okay, and she replied in a trembling voice, trying to fight off the tears that were too good for the likes of a guy like me, "No Nick, it is not."

"What's wrong? Come over here." I said.

"No this will only take a second," she responded. "I want to hear it from you... did you sleep with Joanne during the week I went home for the holidays?"

My immediate response, was "No" I fell back onto the stupid guy code, I used to think was so important to live by, which among other things included these three simple words: deny, deny and of course deny.

"I would never do anything to compromise the integrity of our relationship! You know me, who are you going to believe? Me or some ridiculous rumour? Probably made up by some guy who is jealous of what we have and they don't," I ranted, thinking to myself, "What a good line, keep going." So I did. "I can't believe we are having this conversation! In fact, why would you come over here to accuse me of something, we both know I would never do? You are my girl and there is nobody else. Do I get offers? Yes, but trust me all I think about is you." I remember saying to myself that this might just work, do not tell her, if you do, you will hurt her. I didn't want to hurt her, and after a conversation that went on for hours, I convinced her that it was a silly rumour. I was so convincing that I almost believed it myself.

The truth? She was 100% right. I did cheat on her. I had my opportunity to tell her the truth and set myself free but I let that moment pass. For a time things between us were fine, until I did it again. I thought that since I hadn't got caught the first time, I wouldn't this time either. Except I did get caught and this time I couldn't lie my way out of it. After a long fight, a girl that at one point in her life loved me, looked me dead in the eyes and said, "You are a liar and for that I hate you."

Then she turned and walked away, leaving me on the street to watch her go, knowing that there weren't any words that were going to make things right. It wasn't until years later when we happened to be in the same city, that I got the opportunity to tell her the truth and apologize for my stupidity. Thankfully she graciously accepted. I realized that she had forgiven me a long time ago and that I was the one living with the guilt of both lying and cheating that hurt me. When I was able to voice the truth, I felt a major burden lift off my shoulders, which helped me to move forward with my life.

I did not realize it at the time, but my ex-girlfriend's act of calling me on my infidelity and my lying about it was a blessing. Not only was I lying to her but I was lying to myself. I was going through life wondering if this day would be the day I would get caught, and that is no way to live your life. Sometimes you will have to ask yourself the tough questions:

- Am I the person I want to be?
- What do I have to do in order to be that person?
- Do I live my life with integrity?
- When I make a mistake, do I learn from it?

If you can answer these questions truthfully and not lie to yourself or anyone else, your life will be more full and complete. Remember, no matter how much you know it is going to hurt, tell the truth. It really will set you free.

Tell the truth.

Nick

GET INSPIRED

"A man's life is what his thoughts make of it."
— Marcus Aurelius

Dear brother,

The other day I was told a story of violinist who was 84 years old and still performed concerts all over the world, receiving standing ovations and wonderful reviews. While conducting an interview recently, a reporter asked him, "Why do you continue to practice eight hours a day, seven days a week, at your age? You have accomplished so much in your career. Surely, you can slow your pace down and enjoy your successes." The violinist paused before his answer and then responded, "I have not practiced the violin a day in my life. I play that long because I love playing. I do what I do because I love what I do. If I stop loving the violin, I will stop playing it."

To make the most of your life, I believe that you have to find your inspiration. It could be anything: your family and friends, your critics, your supporters or even your cynics. Who it is or whatever it is that inspires you, use it to get where you want to be. It is okay to dream about what you want your life to be. It is good to have aspirations and dreams and then set goals to reach them. Do not float through life without a direction. People that lack direction will eventually discover, they did not experience their fullest potential. Experience your potential.

It is important to remember that it is never too late to be inspired by something. It is not where you are standing that is important, it is the direction you are heading and the steps you are taking to get there.

Find your inspiration.

Get Inspired.

Nick

If You Don't Have the Words Don't Use Them

"Make the best of what is in your power,
and take the rest as it happens."
– Epictetus

Dear brother,

Sometimes in life, we are faced with a situation where we can't find the right words. If you find yourself in that situation, don't try to force something out because you think you need to. For example, people will go to a funeral or a wake, or run into a person at a later date and think it is their duty to go up to the person and say something.

Saying, "I don't know what to say" is not the answer. A friend of mine lost a loved one. A few days later we were out having a beer, trying to get his mind onto something other than his loss. A mutual friend came over to where we were sitting and said, "Hey man, I don't know what to say." He stood there, lingering, waiting for my friend to respond. Eventually I chimed in with, "thanks for your concern man." He got the picture and left. At the time, that mutual friend really did not know how to react to the loss of a loved one. None of us did.

Sometimes being there beside the person is good enough. The person will take respite in the fact that you are beside them. When I didn't know how to handle the death of a friend of mine, as his birthday approached, I went to the pub on my own and got drunk. About an hour into my day of wallowing, my friend Ambrose walked through the door. He sat down beside me and somberly inquired what the occasion was. I told him, he sat next to me in silence for hours, only speaking to me when I spoke to him.

I never forgot that gesture. I knew that if I needed someone to talk about my loss I could; the fact that I had a friend with me during a difficult time, got me through it. Just Ambrose being there was good enough. We didn't force the conversation, we just sat. He didn't have the words, so he didn't use them, and that was far better than anything he could have said.

Remember this when it is your turn to be there for someone.

If you don't have the words don't use them.

Nick

Put Value in the Things that are Free

Life is a gift; it offers us the privilege, opportunity, and responsibility to give something back by becoming more."
— Anthony Robbins

Dear brother,

Society teaches us that everything has monetary value and that is what is important. We are taught to go to school, work hard and save our money, by doing so we will be set up for the future. More often than not, the money people earn, the type of house they live in, the kind of car they drive or their annual salary defines success. Working hard in life is important and I am not by any means minimizing the value of an honest day's work, or the importance of a pay-cheque. I would like to remind you, there is far more to life than this.

Monetary value cannot be put on your mind, your soul, your body, your hopes, your dreams, your ambition and your intelligence. Monetary value cannot be put on early mornings or late nights, sunsets and sunrises, the air we breathe, and the sights we see. Monetary value cannot be put on the moments shared with loved ones, the love of a child or the feeling you get when the "one" walks into the room for the first time. Intimate moments shared between people are what make life immeasurable. Monetary value cannot be put on the trials and tribulations of life, the sense of accomplishment from a job well done, humanity working together or lending a hand to a stranger in need. These are the things that make life worth living. Monetary value cannot be put on the smell of a newborn, the happiness of birth, nor the sadness of death or the pride you get when your child speaks or walks for the first time.

Money can't buy you character, integrity or conviction. These are things that are learned, and earned, throughout life. These are the things we should value.

Put value in the things that are free.

Nick

You Will Always Have a Choice

"It's our choices that show who we really are,
far more than our abilities."
— Joanne Rowling

Dear brother,

From the moment we wake up to the moment we go to bed, we are faced with choices. Some choices are big, some choices are small, some we have to think about and some we just make. The reality is that we are faced with choices, every day of our life. We are not always going to make the right choice. We all make mistakes due to our decisions, some we can learn from others we can't.

What I have learned through life is that if you can learn from the variety of choices you make, then (good, bad or indifferent) through these choices, you will gain valuable life experience. I am going to share with you an event, which did not give the person involved, the opportunity to learn from the choice he made. However, the choices that were made that night have and will continue to have, a profound effect on the people that were involved in this person's life.

Monday April 4th, 2005, started for me as another work day. My alarm went off and I reluctantly rolled out of bed to begin another work week. I went downstairs, poured some cereal and watched Sports Center as I usually did. I had no idea that a 7:35 phone call would forever alter my world.

I showered, shaved, dressed and was just pouring my coffee when the phone rang...

First, let me tell you about my friend Brad. He was the kind of guy that you always wanted to be around. He was the first to ask how your day was and had a real presence about him. He loved history, was great at hockey and was passionate about baseball and the Cleveland Indians. Brad was a guys guy with a big heart. He was selfless and was adored by his friends and long-time girlfriend, a complete all-round person who was a pleasure to know.

Brad and I lived together at University. We shared many memories. I remember coming home from class, all the windows would be open in the house, Brad would be sitting on the couch with his jacket on, holding a tin foiled hot dog and roasted peanuts watching the game. He would welcome me with a simple, "here's your seat bro," while pointing to the opposite couch. "Do you want a dog?" Of course, I would oblige and we would spend the night watching baseball and laughing at the simplicity of the evening.

Needless to say we enjoyed many University and Varsity events together, which were made even more memorable and enjoyable because of Brad's innate ability to make others around him feel welcomed. Brad left University early for his own reasons but I can say without hesitation, that my own experience was fuller because he was a part of it.

When Brad left, time went by and for one reason or the other, Brad and I lost touch. I guess it had more to do with being busy with our lives than anything else, but as it always does, time goes by. About four months before the early morning phone call, Brad's name popped into my head. I remember thinking to myself that I should call my friend, as it had been way too long. As I write this, I still cannot put my head around what was so important in my life, that I could not pick up the phone to see how my friend was doing. Days turned into weeks, weeks into months and I never found the time to call. I could not spare a few minutes to catch up with a friend of mine.

As the phone rang, I remember looking at the caller ID and when the name of a familiar friend came up, I answered the phone with an exuberant "hello," anticipating the person on the other end to meet my enthusiasm, with an equally energetic response. Instead what I heard was a meek, soft voice, asking if she could speak with me.

As I replied that it was me that she was speaking to, I thought to myself "I can't wait for her to tell me that she and my boy are engaged." I thought it was her telling me because Brad was not much of a phone person. Instead she continued with, "It's Sandra," to which I replied, "I know, how are you?"

"Not good."

"Oh, what's wrong?"

"There has been an accident and Brad is dead."

I felt numb: I didn't know what to say, so I responded with, "Thank you for telling me" and I hung up.

Life up to that point had not prepared me for that news and I did not know what to do. I walked to the basement of the house, so as not to wake any of my roommates and I called my dad. I told him what happened, and he told me to call my friend back.

"What happened?" I said, as soon as I heard her upset voice answer the phone.

Her reply was simple, "A car accident. He was coming home from a get-together."

"Was he drinking?" I asked, knowing the answer before the words left my lips.

"Yes. It was single vehicle crash, he died instantly."

What I am trying to tell you man, is, we all have a choice. I chose not to call my friend for months prior to learning of his death, and now I have to live with the fact I did not connect with him when I should have. Can I learn from that choice? Of course. Have I? Yes. I do my best to reach out to friends, whenever I think of them. Will Brad learn from his mistake? No. His choice resulted in his death. His mom and dad lost a son, his brother lost a brother, his fiancée lost a future husband, his family a relative, and the world lost a young, charismatic gentleman who consistently made the people around him better.

Life is full of choices brother, that's what makes it so great, prepare yourself to make the right ones. My hope is that you will be able to reflect upon this story, when you are faced with a difficult decision.

You will always have a choice.

Nick

BE HAPPY

"Nothing can bring you happiness but yourself."
– Ralph Waldo Emerson

Dear brother,

One of the most important things in life is to be happy. It is a relatively simple five letter word, with a strong meaning. Being happy is essential, if you want to be truly successful in life. The key to being happy is to surround yourself with people that make you feel good, or let you be yourself. Your friends, your children, your family and the company you like to keep are the keys to happiness. People that have your well-being at heart, genuinely make you feel like yourself and give you the freedom to be yourself. These people are very important.

It seems easy enough to be around people that make us happy, yet sometimes we get caught up in a relationship that is not conducive to happiness. The relationship may have started off making you feel happy but somewhere along the way, you lose sight of what it is that makes you feel good. You find yourself being around this person for no other reason than it is familiar, safe and convenient. If you find yourself in a situation like that, as hard as it may be, you need to take control. It may seem difficult at first because you feel you do not know anything else. But I will guarantee you, in the larger life picture you will both be better off.

Do not sacrifice your happiness for anyone. Compromise is important but do not sacrifice your happiness or well-being, to stay in a relationship. Life is way too short to be looking back and thinking, I should have gotten out of this relationship when I realized that I was not happy.

Relationships happen. Some last, some don't. What makes some relationships last and others not? I don't know. I do know if you enjoy the person you have chosen for all their idiosyncrasies and ideologies, you can laugh with that person, feel comfortable enough to share your dreams and goals and look at them like there is nobody else in the room, chances are you are in the right relationship and you will be happy. Do not settle. Settling is the easy way out. You are not ordinary, so don't settle for ordinary, expect the extraordinary, and nothing less.

When you are truly happy, your world will seem exceptionally better.

Be happy.

Nick

Do Not Live with Regret;
Do Not be Afraid to Take Risks

"Those of us who refuse to risk and
grow get swallowed up by life."
— Patty Hansen

Dear brother,

I heard a story once of two little seeds that were lying side by side in the spring soil. The first seed said, "I want to grow, I want to plant my roots deep into the earth's soil, I want to open my buds to the spring sun and take in all of what this beautiful world has to offer." So she grew.

The second seed said, "I am afraid. If I send my roots into the soil below I do not know what I will encounter in the dark. I may damage my sprouts as I push through the soil; a small child may pick me if I unfurl my beautiful blossom. It is much better for me to wait; wait until it is safe." So she waited.

A yard hen scratching the ground, looking for food, found the waiting seed and promptly ate it. As Patty Hansen said, "…refuse to risk and grow, get swallowed up by life."

That moral is true. Life is too short to be living with regret. There will be times in your life when you will come to a crossroads and be faced with a decision: should you take this chance or not? My advice is take the chance and trust your instincts. You are a smart guy. You know the risks that should be taken and the ones that should not. If you want something bad enough go out and get it, do not toil with the thought because by then it may be too late.

Most of the successful people in this world went out and did what they wanted to do because it made them happy. They decided to take a risk, found something they loved and made it happen. Jack Canfield, co-author of *Chicken Soup for the Soul*, had an idea for a book that he felt could be successful. He set a goal, then went out and achieved it. It took hard work, time and dedication, but because of his actions, he has helped millions worldwide, with his heart-felt, feel-good stories. If Mr. Canfield had decided not to take a risk, we would not have been able to enjoy his works and he would have lived his life with the regret, of not doing what he was destined to do.

John Lennon, said "Life is what happens when you are busy making other plans." I know you are a fan and have always admired him. He is a man, who by all accounts lived his life doing the things that he wanted. He took risks with the music he made and the art he produced.

Life is too short not to do the things that make you happy. The last thing you want to say to yourself is, "I wish I would have." If there is something you want to do, then I suggest you do it.

Do not live with regret; do not be afraid to take risks.

Nick

Focus On the Positives Not the Negatives

"Reflect upon your pleasant blessings,
of which everyman has plenty;
not on your past misfortunes of which all men have some."
— Charles Dickens

Dear brother,

A couple of weeks ago, I was in a conversation with a friend of mine and he told me that during business meetings, he always focuses on the positive and lets the negative 'float' by. I asked him what he meant exactly and he used the analogy of a river. He told me that every time he talked to a disgruntled customer, he listened for anything positive that he could concentrate on and focused upon that, rather than the negative.

That strategy got me thinking, I wondered if I concentrated more on the positive things that occur in life rather than the negative, would it enhance my life? I began by writing down the positive things I had accomplished for one particular day. Everything from cutting the grass, to holding the door open for someone, made the list. I did not pay any attention to anything that may be perceived as negative. By doing so, I found that my entire thought process began to change. I automatically started to see things in a positive light. When I applied this to my work, my teaching became more intuitive, focusing upon the positives of my students, rather than the negatives, which resulted in a better atmosphere in my classroom.

I continued to apply this practice to everything I could. At one point our cousin, Brandon and I were working on a business plan.

We got a third party to look at it and tell us what they thought. They said they liked the idea, and that initially it would be difficult to make money, however, over time it looked feasible. My cousin and I later discussed what was said. He asked me what I thought and my response was, "He said he liked the company idea and over time we could make money." Brandon laughed and agreed, as he was thinking the same thing.

I am not suggesting that we should ignore everything someone says if we do not deem it positive. Sometimes constructive criticism is good, especially if you can take that criticism and turn it into something productive that can benefit your well-being.

I have since continued to practice this in everything I do - from work - to family to - relationships and I have found that I am a much happier person. Cutting the negative out of your life is a thought process, so it is important that you are in a positive frame of mind to begin with. When I started to let the negative 'float' by without acknowledgement, I found that I began to live a much happier, more complete life.

Focus on the positives not the negatives.

Nick

KNOW WHEN TO SAY OR NOT TO SAY SOMETHING

"It's better too close your mouth and look like fool,
than to open your mouth and remove all doubt."
— Unknown Author

Dear brother,

Everyone has an opinion and we are always entitled to that opinion. However, there are times, in life when it is best to keep your opinion to yourself and reserve judgment. Too many times people speak their mind without thinking it through. We have all done it: we have all said something and as it leaves our lips, we regret it. Often it is something said in the heat of the moment, something said without thinking, something we blurt out, leaving us scrambling for cover, with stumbled and stuttered phrases that make us look ridiculous.

There is only one practice that can protect you from saying stupid and inappropriate things. It is simple: thinking. That is it. There is no formula, nor is there a special code. If more people would just think before they speak, less people would feel foolish around others. It sounds easy enough to do, but it does take practice. How does one practice this? The next time you are with a group of people and someone says something, before blurting out a response, think it over in your head. If you cringe at the thought of the words you are thinking, then chances are it is not an appropriate response.

There are also times when a person should just listen to the whole story before making a comment. I remember engaging in a conversation with a colleague of mine, as we were sitting at our computers, we began making small talk and before long I realized that he may have worked with a few people I knew. I decided to ask him if he knew a friend of my family, who worked at the same spot. The conversation went exactly as follows:

Me: "Do you know Joe?"

Him: "Yes I do. I hate him."

Me: "Oh I see."

Him: "He is an asshole to work with."

Me: No response.

Him: "We just don't see eye to eye. We have completely different ideologies. He knows his job but is a jerk, every single time I see the way he works, I want to punch him in the face as hard as I can! Man I hate that guy."

Me: "Wow! That's a lot of built up anguish."

Him: "Yeah, well he is an asshole. So how do you know him?"

Me: "He is my uncle."

Him: Awkward pause

Me: "I'll let him know you said hello." I then proceeded to leave the room.

The direction that conversation took could have been entirely avoided, if a little discretion was used. I know and understand that people are not going to like every person that they work with or meet, however, if my colleague had thought to himself, "maybe Nick knows this guy," before answering the way he did, the whole conversation could have been avoided. Here is an example of how that conversation could have happened if a little forethought had occurred.

Me: "Do you know Joe?"

Him: "I do! I worked with him for a few years."

Me: "Oh yeah? He is my uncle."

Him: "We didn't have the best relationship; however, he knows his job."

Me: "Well you can't get along with everyone." Then the subject would be changed.

After that conversation, no one would walk away thinking that the other person was out of line, which in turn would not result in a strained working relationship.

People talking behind the backs of others happens all the time. We have all been victims of it, you have done it and I have done it. Believe me, talking behind someone's back doesn't do anything but make the talker look like a fool. If in life you have something to say to someone, say it to their face. They would much rather hear it from the source, than from somebody who has heard it and passed it on to them.

Something else to remember: (and I am sure that this has been passed down from generation to generation) if you do not have something nice to say, do not say anything at all. I overheard a conversation once that completely shocked me. It went like this:

Girl 1: "Do you know Maria?"

Girl 2: "I do. I went to high school with her."

Girl 1: "Oh that's right I remember her saying that. I think she is such a nice person. I am going to enjoy working with her."

Girl 2: "I am surprised that you would like her."

Girl 1: "Why is that?"

Girl 2: "Well because she is so opinionated. Just the other day she told me she thought you looked fat."

Girl 1: "Oh, well everyone has an opinion." (Clearly trying to make light of the comment.)

The first thing that came to my mind, was what good did that "fat" comment from girl number two do? Did it really need to be brought up that this girl said that? No good could come of it. Not only did she make the young lady feel terrible, she also created animosity between two people. Perhaps the girl didn't want her colleagues to be friends, so that is why she said it, but at the end of the day, she just made herself look bad.

Throughout life, we are faced with times it is appropriate to say something and times it is not. The most common situations where people get tongue tied and awkward are when receiving compliments. Compliments are difficult for some people to take. It could be self esteem issues or it could be that they are just uncomfortable with flattery. The following is a list of what is appropriate to say when receiving a compliment.

1. "Thank you."
2. "That is very nice of you to say."
3. "Thank you."
4. "Thank you."
5. "Thank you."

Inappropriate to say:

1. "You don't mean that."
2. "Whatever."
3. "No I don't."
4. "You say that to everyone."
5. "Someone must have told you to say that."

My hope is that this small list will help give you a blue-print to follow. The important thing to remember in all of this is to think. We are capable of it; we just need to practice it more. Thinking before you speak will make your life much easier. You will be able to cut down on the moments, where you find yourself regretting the words that have come out of your mouth.

Know when to say, or not to say, something.

Nick

MAKE YOUR OWN CIRCUMSTANCES

"The people who get on in this world are the people who get up
and look for the circumstances they want,
and if they can't find them, make them."
— George Bernard Shaw

Dear brother,

If you think about a goal and execute a plan to accomplish that goal, you will be successful no matter the circumstance. Too many times in life, people blame where they ended up, on the people around them or on bad luck. In my opinion, there is no such thing as luck. I am not saying people do not fall on tough times or that bad things do not happen. What I am saying is that the people who experience the most success, respond to what life presents them, optimistically and with the attitude they are going to persevere. They are focused, they do what they have to do, no matter what obstacles life throws in their direction.

Mike was a perpetually happy person who always looked at life with high degree optimism. He was the type of guy that people were drawn to. Mike worked in the restaurant industry as a manager, his employees always said he was the greatest boss and made people feel like they were part of the team. No matter how bad a situation was, his staff had no problems going to him because he was always open and optimistic. He reminded his staff that they always had a choice, no matter what the circumstance.

A few years ago Mike was working late, closing up the restaurant, when the unthinkable happened. Mike was robbed at gun point by two masked men. The two men told Mike to open the safe and as he was doing so, the gun went off striking Mike in the back. The robbers immediately ran off, leaving Mike lying in a pool of blood to die. Mike said, that as he was lying there, two things entered his mind: The first was, "I wish I would have locked that back door." And the second? "No matter what happens, I choose to live!"

Through his willingness to survive, Mike managed to find the strength to call the paramedics. When they arrived, they reassured him that he was going to be okay, constantly telling him, "You are going to be okay, you will be back in shape in no time."

However, when he got to the hospital, the mood seemed to change. He remembered looking up at the doctors and thinking, "They are looking at me as though I am a goner!"

"The doctors were asking him, with urgency stamped on their faces, "Sir! Are you allergic to anything? Sir! Can you hear me?"

Without hesitation Mike responded, "YES!" causing everyone in the operating room to stop. "I am allergic to bullets!"

Immediately everyone in the room started to laugh, which prompted Mike to continue, "I am allergic to bullets, so operate on me as a man who chooses to live, not as a man who is dying."

At that moment Mike knew he was going to survive. Mike recovered fully. This story was told to me by mom, as she remembered it from a book she read.

I use this story to compound my point because it is an example of a person, who didn't let what happened to him cause him to give up. Mike took one of the worst circumstances life could give him and made a decision to live. Anytime in my life I start to feel sorry for myself, I think of Mike's story and quickly realize that I will always have a choice to make my own circumstance. People are always blaming their predicament on the situation, which is occurring around them. Do not be that person! Work hard and do the right thing. You are not a victim of circumstance. Be accountable. Create your own luck.

Make your own circumstance.

Nick

READ

"Reading is to the mind what exercise is to the body."
— Joseph Addison

Dear brother,

Read. Knowledge is power. Education does not start and stop with the beginning and the end of school. Take in as much as life has to offer. The trick to reading is finding something you enjoy, something you are interested in, such as sports, history, fantasy, non-fiction, true crime, etc… The truth is there are enough books in this world that at least one will appeal to you.

Reading should not be a chore. Find time to enjoy it, perhaps before bed, or on the toilet or while traveling. It doesn't matter where or even how often, as long as you do it. Reading expands the mind, opens up endless imaginary and academic possibilities and can provide a reprieve from our everyday.

Trust me. With time you will enjoy it.

Read.

Nick

THERE ARE TWO TYPES OF PEOPLE:
'SAYERS' AND 'DO-ERS'...BE A 'DO-ER'

"The way to get started is to quit talking, and start doing."
— Walt Disney

Dear brother,

There are two types of people in this world: 'SAYERS' and 'DO-ERS.' 'Sayers' are the type of people that have much to say. In fact, these are the people, you hear at parties or in the office, saying, "I am going to do this" or "I am going to do that, I just need to wait for the right opportunity." In reality, said opportunity will never arrive for the Sayers. Instead, Sayers will consistently come up with inevitable excuses, for why they in fact did not take that trip, or go after that job, or follow that dream. From money, to family, to various other circumstances, it will be one excuse after another. This will continue and inevitably, the next time you see that person they will be saying the same things... "I am going to" "eventually" "someday." For Sayers though, that someday will never come. An example of this concept happened in my life.

Years ago, I bumped into an old friend at a bar. After the small talk was over, Jane and I began discussing where we would like to be when we finished school. Jane told me she planned to go South Korea to work. I was thrilled for her and told her it was a great idea to go out, to see the world and experience everything it has to offer. However, two years later I bumped into Jane over Christmas, I inquired if she still planned on going to South Korea. She told me that she would but she had met someone and her plans weren't as definite. Being old friends, I told her that she would regret it if she didn't go and I hoped she followed her dream.

Years passed and Jane never went to South Korea. Instead she decided to stay home, settle down and get married. You might be thinking, so what? What's wrong with that? Maybe that is what she wanted to do! And if that was the case, you would be right and I would agree. However Jane and I crossed paths sometime later, she mentioned her biggest regret in life was that she didn't seize the opportunity of going to South Korea, when she had the chance.

She never went. Jane is a Sayer.

On the contrary, "Do-ers" do the things they talk about. Do-ers are the people who say they are going to do things and have a plan to get it done. I know many do-ers in my life.

When I was in teachers college, my friend Paul, talked about teaching away from Canada, to get some life experience before he decided to settle. One night he sat down with a couple of friends; he thought of all the places he would like to teach and decided on England. That was in May by December of that same year, he found a place to live, found a job and obtained a two-year working holiday visa. He went over and had one of the best experiences his life had to offer. Is he any different than Jane? No. The only difference is that he decided to act. He didn't wait, didn't make excuses and said, "The time is now," he made it happen.

Can Sayers become Do-ers? Absolutely yes! We do things everyday in our life without even thinking about it; we wake up, get out of bed, eat breakfast, shower, brush our teeth and get dressed. We are genetically made up to be Do-ers. That is the best part of becoming a Do-er, we already are! Some just need to become better Do-ers. If we wake up one morning, deciding that today will be the first day of striving to achieve a goal, and start formulating a plan to reach that goal, then we have automatically become a Do-er. The goal does not need to be as big as moving to a different country. It can be anything you want. Start off small, build confidence and prove to yourself, you can do it. From there, you will find that you will be able to accomplish everything you ever wanted to.

There are two types of people: 'Sayers' and 'Do-ers' be a 'Do-er'.

Nick

YOU ARE GOOD ENOUGH

"Strive not be a success, but rather to be of value."
— Albert Einstein

Dear brother,

There are going to be times in your life, when you don't feel very good about yourself. There will be times when you are down and out, even depressed. Believe me when I say those days will pass. I want to tell you that you are good enough. As you go through life, you will come across people who will try to tell you, that you are not good enough. It may not be as profound as that, or stated in as simple terms. It may be subtle hints and nuances that are designed to make you uncomfortable, said to make you lose confidence and get you down on yourself.

I asked many people about the words of advice they would give to their brother. The response I got from a friend of mine - "You are good enough" was interesting. I often got answers from people, having no idea of their background, their prejudices or precursors. In this case though, I did. It was the younger sister of a close friend of mine, a guy I view as a charismatic, strong willed and confident individual. I personally felt he would never struggle with being good enough. However, people do not always present, the way they feel inside.

It would be difficult to imagine the sports world, without basketball great Michael Jordan. Did you know that if he had listened to his high school basketball coach, the one who cut him from the team, we would not have been blessed with his greatness? He was told he was not good enough, but he knew that he was. He took his adversity and turned it into a hall of fame career.

Take pride in the fact that you are you. Be yourself; you are an original. We are all created differently. Let your views and values be your own. Embrace your differences, take pride in who you are and do not forget in a world that is filled with ambiguity, above all else, you are good enough.

You are good enough.

Nick

THINK FOR YOURSELF

"Always be a first-rate version of yourself,
instead of a second-rate version of somebody else."
— Judy Garland

Dear brother,

I want to stress to you the importance of being able to think for yourself. In my life I have come across many people, who do not have an original thought in their head and easily adhere to the masses, for fear of being viewed as an outcast. I see this everyday as a teacher, when a young person with a different ideology from the rest of the class, constantly refuses to add an opinion.

As you get older, you will find being your own person gets easier, I think this occurs because the older you get the more you realize that we are all original. Try your best to be accepting of others, no matter what they believe. You may not agree with every person and their thoughts or opinions but if you can appreciate original thought, then you will value others, if you value others, you will gain respect and tolerance for different backgrounds and beliefs.

The quicker you realize that we are all unique, the more confident you will be in life and the more likely you will be, to understand that life is viewed differently by everyone. Be your own person, do not let others manipulate your thoughts, be original and do not compromise yourself for anyone.

Think for yourself.

Nick

PART FIVE

HEALTH & WELL-BEING

DRESS FOR THE OCCASION

"The finest clothing made is a person's skin,
but of course, society demands something more than this."
— Mark Twain

Dear brother,

There are times in life when you are going to need to dress for the occasion; make sure when that occasion arrives you dress appropriately. Too often I see men at a wedding, a formal banquet or a funeral, and they are under-dressed. Wearing shorts and a t-shirt to a wedding (unless otherwise specified) is an example of being under-dressed. You do not need to be a big city person, working in a high paying job to have a pair of dress pants and a collared shirt.

I am all for a person having their own style and adding their own touches to spice up the suit that they are wearing. However, I think wearing sandals with dress pants is not making a statement, it is screaming that you are trying too hard to go against the norm. Dressing appropriately for the occasion shows that you take pride in yourself, respect the occasion, and respect the person who you are there with.

We do not all have the same style, so if you are not blessed with the gift of being able to put different combinations together, my advice is to keep it simple. Black belt always goes with black shoes. You can put this belt/shoe combination, with pretty much every suit colour. If you are looking for a suit colour for all occasions, the answer is black. Black suits work for weddings, funerals, semi formals, and everything else you could use a suit for. If you are looking for a shirt, my suggestion would be a plain white or blue shirt. Semi-Formal? Lose the jacket. Formal? Put the jacket on and perhaps add a tie. All ties go with back suits and white shirts. Follow those simple suggestions and you will have appropriate attire for all occasions.

Dress for the occasion.

Nick

USE SKIN CREAM

"That which is striking and beautiful is not always good,
but that which is good is always beautiful."
— Ninon del'Enclos

Dear brother,

Wear skin cream. I know you may be thinking huh? You want me to wear what? The truth is, it is important to take care of your skin because we are only on this planet once. I am not sure where the stigma of men taking care of their skin came from, but it is important to do so. Preferably something with an SPF of 15 or higher. It should be applied everyday, during all seasons, with no exceptions.

Skin cancer does not discriminate between gender and age, so you need to protect yourself against harmful UV rays; sunscreens, as well as eye and face creams are available for men. They are helpful for keeping your skin moisturized, which is an important step to keeping your appearance healthy. Find a product that you are comfortable with and use it.

Use skin cream.

Nick

An S.T.I. is an S.T.I No Matter What the Story is

"Quite simply condoms are cool, and using them is cooler.
We want to make it trendy, hip and cool to use condoms."
— Bill Reedy

Dear brother,

Not too long ago, a friend confided in me about the possibility of having contracted an S.T.I. He told me his new girlfriend thought that she may have contracted the infection from her ex boyfriend, who had a history of cheating. The first response that came out of my mouth? "An S.T.I is an S.T.I no matter what the story is." He agreed and later that day, he went to the clinic to get checked.

The point is if you wear a condom, your chance of contracting a sexually transmitted infection is far less likely than it would be if you didn't. I know a lot of men think that it is embarrassing to talk to their physicians about the possibility of sexually transmitted infections, but I say it is far less embarrassing to consult privately with your physician, than to receive a phone call from a (former) partner saying that they have contracted an infection from you. If you are sexually active, it is your responsibility to take care of your health and not put others at risk.

Wearing a condom is important. It protects against infections, disease and unwanted pregnancies. People in our society have to take responsibility for their actions. Using excuses like, "I didn't have one," or "I got caught up in the moment" are cop outs and are signs of immaturity. Wear a condom; it may save your life.

An S.T.I is an S.T.I no matter what the story is.

Nick

DRESS APPROPRIATELY IN AIRPORTS

"Dressing up, people just don't do it anymore.
We have to change that."
— John Galliano

Dear brother,

I have been fortunate enough to travel to many places in my life and I have seen the insides of many airports, in many different countries. That said, I want to let you know when traveling, make sure you dress appropriately. I am not saying shirt and tie but if you are traveling for business, make sure you dress in business like attire. If you are traveling for a vacation make sure you dress practically.

I have found, through my travels that while waiting for planes, you meet many different people and you want to make sure you represent yourself well. In business situations, you are not only representing yourself but also the company you are working for. You want to be dressed like a gentleman, as you never know what conversation may arise while waiting for your plane to take off.

I understand if you are flying to long distances it may not be practical to wear a suit the whole time. My advice is to pack something to lounge in while on the plane, then change into your suit when you have reached your destination.

Many times, I see vacationers traveling wearing sandals and next to nothing on the plane, as most of the time they are going somewhere hot. However, one piece of advice: If you are traveling for vacation purposes, try your best not to wear sandals that are easy to slip off. You want to be prepared for emergencies, so if you must wear sandals wear the type with a back on them, though my suggestion is to wear shoes. You should dress appropriately, while being practical at the same time for vacation and for business.

Dress appropriately in airports.

Nick

GET REGULAR CHECK-UPS

"No Doctor is better than three."
— German Proverb

Dear brother,

You need to get regular health check-ups. Taking time out of your life to see a doctor when you don't feel particularly bad may seem like an inconvenience. Trust me, nobody enjoys a prostate exam or the particulars of a complete physical, but it is necessary and it is a part of living a healthy lifestyle.

As a man, I would rather get regular check-ups, than go to the doctor and find out I have something, which could have been prevented or treated and now has turned into a grave situation. Think of it this way: you take your car to the mechanic every so often to get it serviced or the oil changed, in order for the automobile to run better. Your body is like a machine and as it gets older, it is more susceptible to break-downs and problems. It is better to treat the prospects of problems before they turn into something that is far more serious. Getting a physical is necessary, do not brush it aside as something that you will do when you get older. Get into the habit of doing it young and make it part of your routine, every one or two years.

Get regular check-ups.

Nick

Sleep Late Once in A While

"The amount of sleep required by the average person
is five minutes more."
— Wilson Mizner

Dear brother,

You have heard me suggest many times that there is absolutely no substitute for hard work and effort. However, every once in a while, I think a person needs to sleep in, to relax and not think about all the things they have to do. Life can be very fast paced. Slow it down on occasion by staying in bed.

If you think sleeping in a few extra hours will put you behind for that day, then I suggest you get the next day's duties in order before you go to bed. Sleeping in a little or lying in bed and relaxing, will help you start your day fresh. I am not suggesting that you do this every day, in fact for most of us, this practice is not feasible, due to the responsibilities of work and life. What I am suggesting, however, is that you put this theory into practice at least once a month. Allow yourself some quality bedtime and relax.

Sleep late once in a while.

Nick

TAKE CARE OF YOUR TEETH

"You don't have to brush all your teeth,
just the ones you want to keep."
— Author Unknown

Dear brother,

Your teeth are very important, so make sure you take care of them. Brushing them once or twice a day is not good enough. You should floss every day and brush with the right tooth paste and tooth brush. Make sure that you get dental check-ups, at least every six to nine months. Do not wait until you have a toothache to see the dentist. Be proactive, not reactive, when it comes to your dental hygiene.

Healthy teeth lead to a healthier life. If you take care of your teeth it will reflect in your confidence. A person with a healthy looking smile is a person, who people know takes pride in their appearance and their overall well-being. Going to the dentist can be an intimidating experience, so find a dentist you are comfortable with.

You do not want to be the person that gets older and has none of their own teeth due to negligence. Go to the dentist and educate yourself on how to properly look after your teeth.

Take care of your teeth.

Nick

Take at Least 10 Minutes a Day for Yourself

"For fast-acting relief try slowing down."
– Lilly Tomlin

Dear brother,

Life can be busy. It seems that once one task is completed, another one is ready to begin. It can be overwhelming and it does not get any easier with age. Responsibilities for your job, family, friends and extracurricular activities can take their toll on your health and well-being. I could only imagine that if you add children into the mix, how stretched a person's time can be.

You need to find time in your busy schedule for yourself. It makes no difference if this time is at the beginning of the day, the end, or in the middle. You need to have at least ten minutes so you can collect your thoughts, think about what you need to do and give yourself a sense of balance. Ten minutes is not a long time but if you do it every day, it will help to keep yourself organized and centered. Here are some simple suggestions on how to spend that time.

1. Reading - Find a good book or a magazine to lose yourself in. Reading is a nice reprieve from the fast pace of life.
2. Sitting in silence - Sitting and doing nothing may seem difficult for a busy person, but the effects of mastering the art of having a good sit will help to slow down the pace of your life.
3. Walking - Walking is a great way to think and clear the mind. It gives you an opportunity to clear your head and gather your thoughts.
4. Exercise - Ideally you want to do physical activity a little longer

than ten minutes a day, however, 10 minutes is better than doing nothing at all. Get your heart rate up - you will feel positive effects all day.

5. Listen to music - My favorite thing to do. Put on your head phones or turn the radio up. Listening to music can alter your mood: soothe you when necessary, buoy you when required. It can put you in the frame of mine to accomplish things, or to wind down a manic day.

Ten minutes in a twenty four hour period is a small amount of time, however, the effects of doing this everyday will help your overall well-being and psyche. In turn, this will give you the ability to accomplish your everyday tasks and make you more available for the people in your life, who need you the most.

Take at least ten minutes a day for yourself.

Nick

CPSIA information can be obtained at www.ICGtesting.com
Printed in the USA
LVOW10s2252210314

378442LV00007B/24/P

9 780986 888908